GW00514714

A–Z guide to pet health

In the same series

W.J. Jordan

A–Z guide to pet health

Illustrations by Lindsay Blow

Constable London

First published in Great Britain 1986
by Constable and Company Limited
10 Orange Street London WC2H 7EG
Copyright © 1986 by W.J. Jordan
Set in Times New Roman 9pt by
Inforum Ltd, Portsmouth
Printed and bound in Great Britain
by The Bath Press, Avon

British Library CIP data
Jordan, W.J.
A–Z guide to pet health. (Constable A–Z guides)
1. Pets——Diseases
I. Title
636'.089'6   SF981

ISBN 0 09 465890 0

Preface

by Katie Boyle

Despite many publicised cases of appalling cruelty, I think we can still call ourselves, on the whole, an animal-loving nation. But, to be fair, I would add that we are often ignorant in our love, and so cause untold, if unconscious, misery too. For instance – bringing an unfortunate goldfish back from a fair in a plastic bag with a few inches of unoxygenated water, or mistaking a tumour in a beloved budgie for an unlaid egg, or ignoring a miscarriage in a bitch who you never even knew had dallied on her way!

Love and understanding do not go hand-in-hand when it comes to pet-owning, and Bill Jordan has written a very much needed book. Not only are his knowledge and experience extensive, as a top veterinary surgeon to the RSPCA for many years and now a member of their Council, as well as a hard-working Director of the People's Trust for Endangered Species, but I have also had many an occasion on which to admire at first hand his personal and intensely caring involvement with animals in need.

But please don't buy a copy of this book and leave it on the shelf just in case of an emergency. This is a book to read and get to know, and *then* keep within easy reach. It will teach us all to understand the weaknesses of many animals, and therefore will help us to care much more for the pets we profess to love. It is a riveting and informative book, written by a dedicated man on a subject he knows intimately.

K.B.
1985

Introduction

Pets can be a delight. They can brighten the day and lighten our lives. But they are also a responsibility, because they must depend entirely on us for their well-being. Life is full of such hazards as disease and accident, and pets cannot tell us what is wrong or where it hurts.

We can of course turn to the vet for help. His thorough training and years of experience have equipped him to diagnose and treat most complaints.

But should we take our pet to the vet every time he coughs, gets a cut, or refuses his food? Between treatments, how do we nurse our pet and administer his medicine? What would we do if he has worms? What should he be vaccinated against, and when? Why does he scratch so much? Will he bleed to death? Should his urine be that colour? And what *is* his normal temperature? These are some of the many questions to which we want answers quickly, without having to read half a text-book on animal diseases.

The A–Z format of this book provides easy reference; and to assist the ordinary pet-owner, for whom it is intended, there are many cross-references to make sure all common names are covered. It is *not* a book on home treatments, for the skill and experience of the vet are essential in many instances; but it is intended to help dispel the fear and anxiety which lack of knowledge gives rise to, by explaining the problems, and by giving some indication of the prognosis (the way the course of the disease may go).

Keep this book within easy reach, so that you can refer to it urgently. It will provide you with the answers you need, from A (abscess) to W (wounds).

W.J.J.
1985

Increase in size may be due to fat, pregnancy, fluid, gas, obstruction, worms, enlarged bladder or womb, tumours, blood, or old age.

Over-fat animals are prone to illness. Restrict food intake, particularly carbohydrate, whilst making sure the animal has an adequate intake of protein, minerals and vitamins (see Diet).

Pregnancy is preceded by heat and mating – not always observed (see Pregnancy).

Fluid may be due to heart or liver disease or peritonitis. The animal is ill, often old, and should be taken to a vet at once.

Gas accumulates suddenly from food fermentation or obstruction in the bowel or twisting of the stomach or intestines. It is accompanied by pain and later collapse. In the horse it is called colic. Keep animal walking about and if severe or not relieved in two hours call the vet urgently. If extreme in the dog it may be twist of stomach and surgery is the only treatment. Milder cases can be given milk of magnesia. Cats, rabbits, guinea-pigs and hamsters rarely have this problem.

Obstruction of the bowel by a hard mass of food material may cause distention of the abdomen. If severe, surgery is necessary. If mild, a teaspoon of liquid paraffin twice daily should help. Cats frequently have blockage of lower bowel caused by matted hair (hair ball). Try a teaspoon of liquid paraffin twice daily. If unsuccessful in two or three days, take to a vet. Obstruction can also be caused by twist of intestine, telescoping of bowel, or by foreign bodies. The animal is acutely ill and only the vet can help.

Worms cause pot bellies in young animals. Modern worm remedies are effective and safe if given at the correct dose (see Parasites).

Enlarged bladder (see Bladder).

Enlarged womb (see Womb).

Tumours can affect all species. They are rare in young animals and not common in adults except perhaps the budgie, in which they can be confused with an egg which the bird is unable to lay. In the latter case, lubrication of the passage with liquid paraffin is advised, but it's not the job for an amateur. Fish with distended abdomens are usually full of eggs with which they will have no difficulty.

Blood in the abdomen follows injury – a bite, kick, or run-over accident. The animal is shocked, gums are pale or bluish and a vet is needed urgently.

In old age muscle tone is gradually lost and the abdomen becomes pendulous and appears distended. Use tender, loving care.

Pain in the abdomen is caused by injury to, or inflammation of, the abdomen wall or any of the enclosed organs. If touched, the abdominal wall will tense and the animal show signs of pain (see Pain). Don't touch your fish. If it's absolutely necessary, use a soft wet cloth or wet hands. Remember the scales are covered with a sensitive transparent membrane.

Enlargement of the abdomen in fish may be due to egg formation in the female, or infection, or internal parasites, or tumefaction following feeding with blood worms, or fluid (dropsy), or tumours. Keep a careful watch for other symptoms and consult the vet should they develop, as a fifth die (see Parasites, Tumours, Quarantine).

ABORTION

Premature birth can occur in all species of animals (not birds or fish). In early stages of pregnancy it may pass unnoticed. When near full-term, it can cause illness. Sometimes serious in the larger species. Watch carefully and if the foetus or foetuses are passed without difficulty and the animal does not appear ill you need do nothing. Otherwise call the vet. Afterwards wash and disinfect the animal and its house and give clean bedding (see Disinfectants). If discharge from vagina persists for a week and animal is not ill, take to a vet.

ABSCESS

A localised infection with pus-forming bacteria contained by the body's defences. It can vary in size from a pimple to a large swelling that is usually hot, painful and containing poisonous material. The commonest site is in or under the skin, less commonly in the muscles or internal organs. Some infections produce a toxin which causes illness and fever with a rise in temperature (see Temperature). In most cases the swelling bursts, discharges pus and heals like an open wound. This natural healing process can be

helped by bathing abscess in hot water with Epsom salts or table salt
added (one teaspoon to a cup of water). Bathe frequently.
Alternatively a poultice can be used according to manufacturer's
instructions. Once the abscess bursts (normally in 5–7 days), treat as
an open wound (see Wounds). If the animal is ill and has a fever, or
the abscess doesn't burst, or there is doubt about the diagnosis, take
the animal to a vet.

Internal abscesses are for the expert to diagnose and treat. They
can interfere with the functions of the organs and symptoms vary.

A pimple is a tiny abscess often caused by an insect bite. It can
become large, but usually large abscesses result from animal bites or
scratches or wounds – particularly puncture wounds.

Not all swellings are abscesses – see Blood blister (haematoma),
cysts and tumours.

Abscesses can develop in tortoises from wounds in any soft tissue.
They are common and can be serious. The contents may be white
and creamy, but more often are hard and cheesy. It is best to open
and carefully remove the contents and *all* dead (necrotic) material.
The cavity is then cleansed thoroughly with a mild antiseptic such as
Iodophor in a weak solution, and a broad-spectrum antibiotic
ointment applied. The wound must be kept open and draining until
it has healed from the bottom. A good diet and unstressful
surroundings are essential.

ACCLIMATISATION

Tortoises will never acclimatise to British weather, so proper
accommodation must always be provided (see Accommodation).
This is because they are poikilothermal animals, i.e. they cannot
produce body heat by shivering, nor adequately lose heat, but are at
the mercy of the environmental temperature.

The most important factor in fish is temperature. A sudden
change of water temperature will cause severe stress. Always check
water with a thermometer. Other factors are PH (acid/alkaline
level), hardness, and salinity (where applicable) of the water.

Never put a newly acquired fish straight into your tank. Always
quarantine it first to prevent spread of diseases (see Quarantine,
Water).

ACCOMMODATION

The tortoise most commonly kept in Britain is one of the three species found in the Mediterranean region. Because they are adapted to a milder winter, accommodation must vary between summer and winter. For it is important to remember that tortoises are cold-blooded (poikilothermal), meaning that they produce very little body heat and have to rely on the environment. When they are too cold they move into the sun and when too hot, into the shade. They are adapted to sandy, peaty soil.

For summer mark out an area of garden that is not prone to flooding measuring about 50 square feet (4.6 square metres). Remove the top soil to the depth of a foot. Remove sharp rocks and litter and line around the edge with bricks to stop the tortoise from burrowing out. Then put in a layer of silver sand with some peat added. Fence the sides with Perspex or solid wood boards, *not net wire* which is very dangerous to tortoises: they may try to climb it and get stuck or fall on their backs. The fence should be sunk into the soil alongside the bricks and be 18 inches (45.7 cm.) high. Provide shade in one corner – a wide high board or a shrub. A shallow pan of water one inch (2.5 cm.) deep should be provided in the pen for bathing and drinking. It must be sunk in the sand so that the side is at ground level. Tortoises cannot bend their heads over and down nor can they suck up water. To complete the accommodation, provide a small wooden box two feet square and two feet deep (61 × 61 × 61 cm.) which is weatherproofed and raised two inches (5 cm.) above the ground. It must have a ridged ramp for access with an open doorway measuring one foot square (30.5 cm.) and containing about one or two inches (5 cm.) of sphagnum moss and scattered leaves and bark for the tortoise to hide under.

It is a good idea to heat the box with a 60-watt bulb about 12 inches (30.5 cm.) above the floor. Tortoises don't like light in the den so darken bulb with non-toxic vegetable-based paint. Provide fresh drinking water in a shallow pan inside the box under the bulb. Test the temperture of the box on both cold and hot days. It should never fall below 65°F (18°C) nor rise above 85°F (29°C).

For winter-time outside accommodation is unsuitable. Indoor accommodation has to be kept to around 78°F (26°C). Old carpet

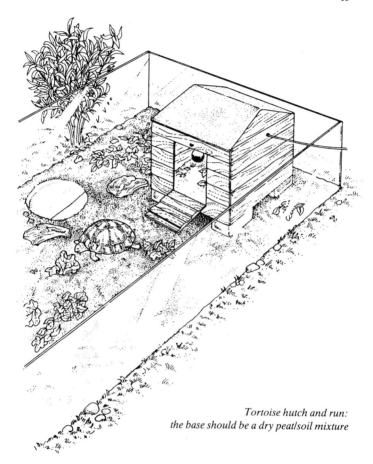

Tortoise hutch and run:
the base should be a dry peat/soil mixture

with newspaper on top for easy cleaning is satisfactory. A waterbath held with low flat rocks around it to eliminate the rim, a 60-watt light bulb hanging a couple of feet (about 60 cm.) above the floor to act as an artificial sun, and a square yard (90 − 90 cm.) of sandpaper tacked to the floor, on which the tortoise can wear down its nails, complete the winter accommodation except for bringing in the heated box.

If a tortoise's temperature drops below 65°F (18°C) its metabolism slows down, it becomes torpid and won't eat. And, worse, the food in its stomach and intestines will begin to decompose, producing gas and toxic material.

For other pets, see Housing.

AERATION

Air is pumped down to the bottom of the fish tank. Greater effect is obtained if it is passed through a diffuser to make smaller bubbles. This allows more fish to be kept in a tank. The main purpose is to circulate the water, bringing deeper water to the surface where gaseous exchange (release of carbon dioxide and uptake of oxygen) occurs. Very little gaseous exchange occurs at the air bubbles.

It may be combined with a filter system (see Filtration).

AGE

Life expectancies of pets are on average:-

Horse	25 years
Donkey	35 years
Dog	14 years
Cat	18 years
Rabbit	4 years
Hamster	2 years
Guinea-pig	3 years
Budgie	18 years
Goldfish	10 years
Tortoise	Can live for 20 years or more, but usually much less in captivity

Old age is not a problem in the wild: predators see to that, when the animal can no longer escape or defend itself. Pets are safe from that fate and, like human beings, gradually deteriorate in the last few years or months, except for hamsters and budgies which seem to remain active till they die. As animals get old their diet should be adjusted. Dogs and cats need less animal protein and more roughage and vegetable protein which they can metabolise better. Dogs and cats don't often have dental decay but they accumulate tartar which should be removed. So it is not necessary to give soft food. Chronic heart disease and kidney disease may become a problem and a diet of more vegetable material and less red meat will help. Later, vision may be less acute and hearing may be affected but the ears should be examined for wax and possible infection. Stiffness of limbs may also be seen.

Remember the fat dog or cat ages sooner.

Horses and donkeys, if properly cared for, will enjoy old age, with perhaps just a little stiffness. Two problems need regular attention. As their teeth wear down there is a tendency for the outer edge of the upper molar teeth, and the inner edge of the lower, to become sharp and damage the cheek and tongue and make chewing difficult. They require rasping by the vet. The other problem is more common because the horn of the foot (like our finger nails) keeps growing throughout life. In the wild it would wear on hard ground. But old animals are less active, are kept in small paddocks anyway and the ground is usually soft grass. So regular trimming by the farrier every six to eight weeks is essential. Otherwise the hoof will turn over, crack and become infected and certainly cause pain.

It is impossible to estimate the age of a tortoise. It was thought that rings on the carapace (top part of the shell) indicated age, but it has now been accepted that this is not correct. The rings have more to do with fluctuation in nutrition.

Because fish continue to grow in size, a rough estimate of their age may be obtained that way. As fish get old the growth rate slows, and they become sluggish. Larger species may live to 20 or 30 years and smaller species may only live for 4 years.

ALLERGY

Hypersensitivity to a variety of substances. Symptoms depend on the organs affected. If lungs – hay fever or asthma-like symptoms develop (see Asthma). If intestines – diarrhoea results (see Diarrhoea). The skin – most commonly affected part – is usually inflamed and sensitive. The animal scratches and rubs; exudation may follow and the skin becomes raw with self-inflicted trauma. Usual causal agents are in the food or from insect bites or stings, pollen, or parasites in carpets or bedding material. It is one of the causes of eczema and dermatitis (see Eczema and Dermatitis).

Another type of skin allergy is Urticaria or Hives. Small areas of skin swell to size of a split pea or a bean and swellings are scattered over part or all of the body. They are firm and itchy: unless severe, the animal will recover in several hours or next day.

The most severe and dangerous allergy is called Anaphylaxis and is not common. Usually caused by injection of foreign materials, e.g. vaccines or serum. Onset is sudden – vomiting, diarrhoea and collapse. Take animal to vet at once for without treatment it may die.

ALOPECIA
See Hair, loss of.

AMOEBIC INFESTATION
Is not uncommon in tortoises, where it is thought to cause little or no harm. But it is a serious infection of other reptiles so care must be taken in a mixed vivarium. When amoebas cause diarrhoea in tortoises it can be treated with dimetranidazole (Emtryl M&B) given by injection at a dose of 75mg/kg.

ANAEMIA
Is a shortage of haemoglobin, the red part of blood – either a shortage of cells or of the red haemoglobin in the cells. There are many causes: repeated blood loss due to bleeding from wounds or sores or ulcers, or to blood-sucking parasites, or to Warfarin poisoning; damage to the red blood cells due to blood parasites or poison such as some metals or coal tar; interference with the productoin of red blood cells due to deficiency of iron, copper cobalt and/or vitamins B12 and C, and also due to some diseases. Symptoms are paleness of the mucous membranes and

breathlessness, and, if severe, weakness and tiredness. Because there are so many causes the owner can only make sure the diet is not deficient and rely on the vet for diagnosis and treatment (see Diet, Minerals and Vitamins).

ANOREXIA
See Appetite, loss of.

ANTIBIOTICS
Are extracts of moulds and suchlike that are capable of preventing the growth of germs, and sometimes they will even kill germs that cause disease. Only very small quantities are necessary and these substances are not as a rule harmful to the animal. Since the first one, penicillin, was discovered a great number have come on to the market, as no one antibiotic attacks all germs. Even then not all germs are susceptible to antibiotics. So it is important to choose the correct one and give it in the correct dose for the right length of time. Nowadays most can be given by mouth, but some have to be injected, and in some diseases it is necessary to inject to get the antibiotic circulating in the body to have maximum effect.

All are on prescription only.

ANUS
Some species have glands beside the anal ring whose purpose is to scent-mark the faeces. In the dog and, to a lesser extent, the cat, the glands become blocked and fill up, causing swelling and irritation. The dog sits its anus on grass or carpet and drags itself along in an attempt to get rid of the material. Sometimes becomes infected and forms abscesses. Prevent by giving adequate roughage in diet (see Diet). The glands can be emptied manually by gripping deep behind gland with finger and thumb and 'milking' backwards, squeezing out the evil-smelling material. Probably best left to the vet.

Tumours can cause localised swelling of the anus.

Protrusion of bowel through the anus (prolapse) occurs in young animals. Continual straining to pass faeces is caused by a blockage at anal ring with hard material. Give liquid paraffin for lubrication – about half a teaspoonful for 10 lbs (4.5 kg.) body weight twice daily for all small pets.

APPETITE

Though appetite is not satisfied for long, wild animals rarely over-eat. A full stomach is not conducive to successful hunting, and wild herbivorous animals never have the opportunity to eat large amounts of concentrates. An insatiable appetite beyond normal may be a symptom of tape-worm infestation in dogs and cats, or of diabetes. Loss of appetite is abnormal and a symptom of many disease conditions. Notice whether the loss of appetite was gradual or sudden, to help the vet diagnose the problem. Don't forget that animals do *not* like a change in diet and some may refuse the new food. Stick to the diet your animal likes provided it is balanced (see Diet). Don't be tempted to give something 'for a change' – it may not be eaten and at worst may cause a digestive upset.

Depraved appetite (horses may eat earth, stones, the bark of trees, paint off buildings, etc.) may be a sign of deficiency of minerals or roughage in the diet, or simply boredom. Foals may eat their mother's faeces to get digestive bacteria. Young dogs also eat faeces, a distasteful habit that they drop as they mature. Prevent them, as they may pick up worms or disease.

Rabbits and birds eat faeces normally – allow them to do so for it is necessary for proper digestion and nutrition.

Tortoises normally have a good appetite and eat a variety of foods – see Diet. Loss of appetite can be caused by an environmental temperature that is below 68°F (20°C), by disease (see Disease, Mouth, Enteritis), egg binding (see Egglaying), and parasites. Make sure the environmental temperature is high enough. Consult your vet for diagnosis and treatment.

The appetite of fish should always be good for they have small stomachs and eat often. (Their stomachs are about the size of their eye.) Lack of appetite is a sign of ill health. Look for other symptoms.

ARTHRITIS

Simply means the inflammation of a joint causing disuse or non-use due to pain and/or stiffness. Limbs of animals are most often affected and noticed because of lameness. Not all lameness is caused by arthritis. Injury to muscles, ligaments and bones also causes lameness.

The causes can be: a simple injury (a knock or twist); a joint poorly formed from birth which is more susceptible to wear and tear; a dietary imbalance causing faulty formation; an infection; a hereditary disease (as opposed to a simple malformation). If lameness is prolonged beyond a week, or severe, take animal to vet for diagnosis which may entail X-ray. Pain is nature's way of ensuring that an injured or diseased part is rested to prevent further injury, and so pain-killers are not so often recommended for animals as they cannot easily be made to rest when the pain has been removed.

Arthritis is more common in dogs than any other pets, perhaps because of their ebullient nature. Cats do become lame but not often because of arthritis. It is seldom seen in other pets, possibly because they have less opportunity to become injured. Sometimes a budgie's overgrown claw can get caught in the furniture of the cage and in its struggle to get free a leg can get twisted and cause arthritis. Usually it will clear up in a few weeks without treatment.

Stiffness of the joints can occur in old age and this chronic arthritis is much more common in dogs than any other pet. Dogs are also susceptible to hereditary defects which can end in arthritis. It is important when buying a puppy to ask for a certificate stating that the pup does not have hereditary defects in its ancestry.

BACK

An arched back or a stiff back is a sign of arthritis of the spine or slipped disc. It will be stiff and immovable. Some animals appear to have arched backs when they are in very poor condition.

A broken back, the result of an accident, normally causes paralysis of the hind limbs and a slipped disc sometimes does too.

For sores on the back, see Dermatitis.

BALANCE

Fish keep upright in the water by sensing balance in the labyrinth, which is a system of organs like those in man. These are also concerned with hearing, for it has been shown that fish can hear.

The lateral line – a line of pressure-sensitive organs running along each side of the body – is used to keep stationary in flowing water.

BALDNESS
See Hair, loss of, and Feathers, loss of.

BANDAGING
Is used to protect an injured area, control haemorrhage, keep treatments in place, and give support. The bandage should be applied firmly enough to remain in place, but not so tightly that the normal blood circulation is reduced or stopped. First apply gauze, then a thick pad of cotton wool (¼ inch or so thick) which makes bandaging easier. Then wind the wool or cotton bandage around the part, each turn of the bandage overlapping the previous one (see diagrams).

BEHAVIOUR
Much is inherited in animals, some is learned. For example, young wild carnivores try to hunt but have to be taught how by their mother. So repeated, patient training of your pet is essential for its well-being and your comfort. Begin once the animal is weaned – or even before if possible, for best results (see Training). Abnormal behaviour can result from lack of proper training and can be caused by distress.

Soiling the house with urine and faeces by an animal that is house-trained is usually due to boredom and frustration, or a change in routine with the animal getting much less attention. Biting and scratching the furniture have similar causes. Cats need a scratching block on which to clean their paws. If you don't provide one they may use your favourite chair. Continual barking or barking when the phone rings, or when people are talking, is due to lack of training and the animal seeking attention which then becomes a bad habit.

Hypersexuality results in certain animals from boredom and lack of attention by the owner.

Excessive fear and other phobias are learned experiences in susceptible animals. Vomiting after food may be a habit developed

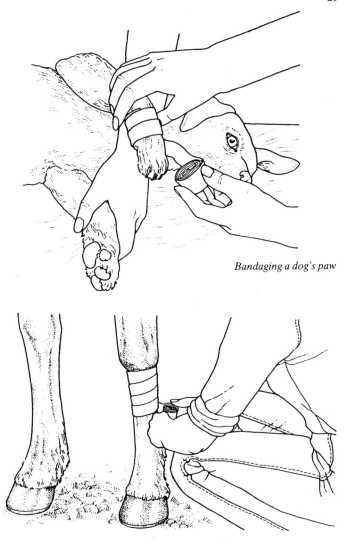

Bandaging a dog's paw

Bandaging a horse's leg

in seeking attention.

Eating grass is normal but if excessive may denote indigestion or faulty diet.

Excessive self-grooming or self-mutilation which is common in zoo animals is occasionally seen in dogs and birds kept in small cages continuously without receiving attention. Parrots are particularly prone to do this and may pull out all their feathers.

Horses that are continuously housed and receive little attention may develop certain bad habits, e.g. crib-biting, when the animal chews the doors and manger and wears down its front teeth.

Wind-sucking (thought to follow crib-biting) when the horse sucks air into its stomach. Both vices lead to loss of condition. Many treatments have been tried but none is thought to be successful. Kicking the stable door continually is another common vice.

Treatment for all acquired behaviour abnormalities is a prolonged period of re-training requiring time and patience.

Behaviour abnormalities due to disease are:

(a) fits and hysteria due to brain tumours and some diseases affecting the brain, e.g. distemper in the dog.

(b) tetanus, when the animal's muscles become stiff and the limbs extended at the slightest stumble.

(c) chorea in the dog, which is a regular twitching of some muscles.

Abnormal behaviour in tortoises can be caused by sexual frustration (see Sexual Frustration); by boredom (see Boredom); by lowering of the environmental temperature (see Temperature); by deformation of the shell, restricting leg movements (see Shell); and by unsuitable ground conditions. The latter can cause abnormal walking movements – legs, usually hind legs, dragged or splayed. The claws may be long and twisted or straight and unevenly worn. The cause is that the ground covering is too soft and deep, and lacks abrasiveness. Treatment: change ground covering and have claws clipped to more normal length. Care is needed, don't take off too much as the sensitive core will bleed. (See Accommodation).

If the tortoise is found frequently overturned, the cause may be the fencing, probably wire, that the animal tries to climb, or the surface may be too uneven, or males may be fighting. (See

Accommodation and Housing).

Stiff legs can be caused by constipation (see Constipation).

The behaviour of fish depends on the species and is a difficult but interesting study. Abnormal behaviour such as flashing or darting about or floating, or continual gulping at the surface of the water and swinging lopsidedly or in a circle, or seeming to be breathing abnormally, or even jumping out of the tank, is caused by water and temperature abnormalities, and by disease and parasites. (See Water, Temperature, Disease, Parasites).

BIRTH

Smaller species of pets can become pregnant and give birth without the owner knowing. They usually give birth unaided. Simply give them a snug box of bedding and leave them alone, (away from their own companions too) quiet and undisturbed. Very occasionally there may be a problem – the female may appear to be ill or there may be a membrane hanging from the vagina. Take her to a vet.

Dogs and cats, especially those who receive constant attention and are having their first litter, require both solitude and reassurance that you are there. Give them an enclosed box in the kitchen or utility room so that they know that you are around. Should the animal be continually straining and no young be born, or should one or more be born and the animal still go on straining, then seek professional help.

After the birth, which is accompanied by slightly bloodstained fluid, you may wish to change the wet bedding. Take the mother away out of sight while this is done or she may get agitated. Thereafter until the young ones' eyes are open and they are moving freely, at about 10 days old, the bedding need not be changed. Mother will keep them clean by licking up their faeces, which is quite normal. From this age onward the mother will usually be quite happy for you, the owner, to caress her young ones.

Horses and donkeys usually have one foal. Give the mother a quiet, well-bedded box large enough for her to lie down and stretch out. As the birth day approaches the mammary glands will enlarge, and about two or three days before the birth the teats will wax, i.e. a small drop of waxy material appears at the end of the teat. It is important to watch unobserved – through a crack in the stable wall. A membranous sac will appear at the vulva, grow larger, and eventually burst, at which time the feet, usually the front feet, appear. From then on birth usually takes an hour or two. If the animal strains continuously and after that time the foal does not appear to be coming out, a vet should be called. Horses are subject to infection of the womb if birth is abnormally delayed. Should only one foot and the nose appear, call the vet.

Once the foal is born the cord breaks and will not bleed. In humans the cord is tied and then cut, but this is not necessary in animals. A membrane (the afterbirth) left hanging from the vulva will rapidly separate from the womb and the mare will strain and pass it. Some animals try to eat this and could choke. So remove it.

If the mare has not got rid of the afterbirth two or three hours after the birth, call the vet at once, for it could set up a serious infection of the womb.

Hygiene is important. Before the birth the vulva and tail region should be washed in soap and water (not detergent). The area should be washed again the day after the birth. Smaller animals keep themselves clean: all the owner need do is provide clean bedding.

BITES

There are two sources of bites – from insects which will be described under Parasites, and from animals.

Under certain circumstances any pet, except fish, will bite. It may happen when animals meet: for example, two dogs in the street or a dog brought to another dog's home; or a cat and a dog; and of course when cats and dogs meet what they think are prey animals – hamsters, rabbits and guinea pigs. At certain times normally placid animals will bite: for example, when angry or frightened, on heat, or guarding their young. When dominant animals meet they may fight: for example, two male rabbits, guinea pigs or hamsters, or two females of those species. Males and females may bite each other when brought together for mating. All introductions should be done slowly and either on neutral ground or in the home of the more docile animal. Treat all situations between animals as potential opportunities for one to bite the other until you have made quite sure they are friendly. Horses will bite each other, donkeys are less prone to do so. But in their case, far more damage is done by kicking.

The majority of bites are puncture wounds. The remainder are lacerations, and sometimes large flaps of skin are torn back leaving raw muscles exposed.

As well as wounding, bites may bruise muscles or break blood vessels, causing either obvious haemorrhage or bleeding within the tissue. This type is more serious and takes longer to heal. If the animal is in a state of shock, or a large area is damaged, or a big swelling has occurred, take it to a vet. Otherwise treat as described under Wounds. Remember the teeth of animals usually carry bacteria and there is a danger of the wound becoming infected. Attend to the bite wound at once and with care.

BLADDER
It is not common for problems to arise with this organ. Occasionally stones develop in the bladder, and sometimes tumours. They will be diagnosed and dealt with by the vet. Frequent passing of urine, and difficulty in passing urine, will be described under Urine.

BLEEDING
See Wounds.

BLINDNESS
See Eye.

BLOAT
Swelling of the abdomen (see Abdomen).

BLOOD BLISTER
Is an accumulation of blood in the tissues or just under the skin, due to the rupture of an artery or vein. It most commonly occurs in the ear flap of dogs and cats and it is usually self-inflicted because of ear canal infection which the animal continually scratches. There is swelling but no excessive heat such as that caused by an abscess. If

the swelling is small, just bandage the ear to prevent further damage, and, most important, examine the ear canal and treat if infected with ear parasites, or if full of wax (see Ear and Parasites). If large, it requires an operation by the vet.

Blood blisters (called haematomas) elsewhere are caused by an injury or bite or kick, or an accident. If small, they will usually be absorbed in time so long as the skin is not broken. Otherwise they may become infected and form a large abscess. If the blood blister is large it can be drained by the vet. Don't attempt to do this yourself, it must be done surgically.

BONES
Broken, see Fractures

BOREDOM
A tortoise that is not given suitable accommodation of sufficient size, and one or more companions, will become bored. It may continually try to climb out of its run and also appear restless.

BREATH
Is normally odourless or nearly so. Bad breath is a sign of ill health. It may be caused by teeth problems, by chronic indigestion, by inflammation or ulcers in the mouth or inflammation of the stomach or kidney disease. A sickly sweet smell indicates acidosis.

Accumulation of tartar on the teeth with accompanying decay of lodged food particles is the most common cause of bad breath, and the animal may not appear to be ill. Kidney disease, which is common in older dogs, makes the animal drink a lot. Indigestion will have other symptoms (see Indigestion). Inflammation of the gums or mouth, or ulcers, will cause local pain and the animal will be 'out of sorts'. Inflammation of the stomach will cause illness and often vomiting. In all cases it is necessary to consult a veterinary surgeon.

Teeth and mouth problems can be prevented by feeding a proper diet. Kidney disease can be vaccinated against (see Vaccine).

Difficulty in breathing can be caused by a sudden allergic response – asthma – caused by the allergens pollen, fungus, dust, etc. And a bite by a poisonous snake or a sting may also cause difficulty.

A foreign body in the larynx or trachea is not uncommon.

Heat stroke in the summer is common (see Heatstroke). Other causes are shock, drowning, various infections besides bronchitis and pneumonia, and accidents that cause internal bleeding or rupture the diaphragm. Some poisons can cause breathing difficulty.

Chronic difficulty in breathing may be due to long-standing disease of the lungs or the heart or some tumour formation. In all cases it is wise to consult the vet. In the horse a special form of difficulty is dealt with under Broken Wind.

BREEDING

See also Pregnancy and Heat.

Tortoises begin courtship in March and continue throughout the summer. The male follows the female everywhere with biting, butting and squeaking. Make sure they are not both males fighting (see Sexing).

Gestation can take from two weeks to four months, during which the female increases in weight and appears restless and may dig holes in a suitable site (loose sandy soil) and lay between one and 15 white, slightly oval eggs very quickly and then leave them. After one mating the female can store sperms for long periods, so if she has not mated recently the eggs can still be fertile.

Eggs can hatch in Britain outside in good summers. It is better to move them to an incubator. Great care is needed not to jolt the eggs and mark the top for they *must not* be turned.

For an incubator use a plant propagator 12 × 18 inches (30.5 × 45.7 cm.). Fit a 15–25 watt bulb for heat and use a mixture of fine sand and peat 3:1 by volume, and make a bed 4 inches (10 cm.) deep in a plastic box measuring 7 × 7 × 5 inches (17.7 × 17.7 × 12.7 cm.). This bedding should be moist but not wet. Place a thermometer on top of soil, close the lid and put container inside the propagator. The temperature should not fall below 75°F (24°C) or rise above 86°F (30°C). Check temperature often and spray bedding with water using an atomiser to keep moist. Eggs take between 8 and 20 weeks to hatch.

Hatchlings are delicate and one or two will die within 24 hours.
Keep in incubator with sand/peat bedding in a warm place (not too
hot) or make an incubator with its own heat source (a 60 watt bulb).
The temperature must not drop below 68°F (20°C) or rise above
85°F (29°C).

Young growing tortoises benefit from sunlight. Provide a shallow
dish sunk in bedding for bathing with water half an inch (1.3 cm.)
deep. Change water daily.

They will grow to 4 inches (10 cm.) long by two years of age.

Feeding – see Feeding.

BROKEN WIND

Is the name given to a condition (emphysema) of the lungs,
generally in older horses or donkeys. The animal has a cough and
difficulty in breathing – it appears to pull up its abdomen to breathe
out. The condition can sometimes be alleviated, but not cured.
Consult your vet.

BRONCHITIS

Is an inflammation of the bronchii – the tubes that join the windpipe
to the lung tissue. It may be acute or chronic and the animal will
cough.

There are several causes – infection by bacteria or viruses or
parasites; irritation by dust and smoke, and continual barking in the
dog. The animal may or may not have a raised temperature. The
safest thing is to consult your vet. If the cough is slight and not too
frequent, a human cough medicine can be tried for a few days so
long as the problem is not worsening. Dose size and frequency is
according to the directions on the bottle scaled down to
bodyweight.

BRUISES

Result from injuries, e.g. bites, kicks or knocks. Tissues are
damaged, tiny blood vessels are broken and enough blood escapes
to discolour the area. Healing will take 10 days or more depending
on size of bruise. The area is painful and warm but not unduly hot.

Keep a careful watch for it is liable to infection especially if the skin is broken, in which case the area should be gently washed with soap and water and antiseptic, or, better, antibiotic ointment applied.

BURNS

May be caused by heat or chemicals or electricity (man-made or lightning) or excessive cold.

The skin is inflamed and painful. Soon blisters will form which burst leaving a raw surface that is slow to heal. If a large area is affected the animal loses fluid and becomes dehydrated, which endangers its life. The animal is shocked if the cause is heat or electricity (see Shock).

When the cause is heat, the application of cold packs will reduce or remove the pain. If the burn is large or the skin is charred or white (third degree burn), go at once to your vet. If it is small and not third degree, stop the cold packs in half an hour or so and apply a loose dry dressing. Do not burst the blister, and treat the animal for shock (see Shock).

If the burn is chemical, wash it away under cold running water. It may take 10 to 20 minutes to be sure it is all removed. If possible wash the area with a shampoo, then cover with a dry loose dressing and if necessary treat for shock.

If the cause is electricity or lightning strike, then the main problem is shock.

If the pet has bitten through an electric wire, or may be still touching a live wire, turn off the electricity at the main before you do anything else. If the animal is not breathing, give artificial respiration by breathing forcefully into its nose while holding its mouth closed, and inflate its chest, then allow air to come out and repeat again at once. Massaging chest over the heart can start a heart that has stopped. There is no time at this stage to take it to a vet. But you can keep the pet alive by giving artificial respiration, provided the heart is beating while the vet is coming to your home.

Excessive cold has to be deep freeze temperature or below and it is unlikely to be a hazard.

CANCER

Is an abnormal growth of cells in any part of the body. It can occur in all species of pets and is uncommon in young animals. There are several types but all that need be noted here is that there are fast-growing cancers that soon cause serious illness and endanger life, and the slow-growing tumours that can be removed surgically with a good prognosis.

Cancer is not common in the horse and donkey.

The two most obvious types of tumours are (1) the swelling and thickening of skin caused by physical damage, namely proud flesh which sometimes occurs with wound healing and lick granuloma caused by constant licking of an injured area; and (2) mammary tumours occurring in the mammary glands of bitches. They are usually not serious but consult your vet.

Cats can get an infection called Cat Leprosy causing single or several lumps in the skin. It is usually not dangerous or serious but again consult your vet.

Guinea pigs get lumps in the neck region which are not tumours but are an infection causing deep abscesses.

Rats and mice get tumours which can be removed surgically.

CANKER

Is a name given to infection of the outer ear canal (see Ear).

It is also a term used for a yellowish growth in the mouth of tortoises (see Mouth).

CARAPACE

This is the dome-like top part of the shell of the tortoise.

CASTRATION

Is the removal of the testicles to prevent breeding and the development of male characteristics that may cause problems, such as fighting other males, and the strong odour of the male cat. It also makes the animal easier to handle. Horses and cats are the species most usually castrated and then perhaps dogs. Smaller animals are rarely if ever castrated.

The operation requires an anaesthetic – preferably a general anaesthetic though some vets use only local. The scrotum is opened to remove the testicles and may or may not be sutured afterwards. The operation takes only 10 minutes or so and the animal is kept quiet afterwards and observed for bleeding or swelling, when the vet must be informed. Healing takes about 10 days. During this time the animal should be fed normally. The animal should be given a clean bed to minimise the chance of infection. There is no doubt that castration changes the character of the animal. But that doesn't mean the animal's temperament and character may turn out to be objectionable. Indeed, it may be more easily trained. There is a tendency for castrated animals to put on weight – which is one of the main purposes for castrating male cattle. However, a good diet will prevent obesity.

CATARACT
Is an opacity of the lens which can be clearly seen in the eye (see Eye).

CAUSTIC DAMAGE
Dogs, cats, and horses can sometimes be contaminated with strong acid or alkali from batteries or bottles of paint-remover, etc., and the injury to body tissues caused by such caustic substances can be severe if not treated immediately. It is important to wash away the chemical carefully before treating the injured area.

CHEST
This houses the heart and lungs. Therefore wounds to the chest are extremely dangerous. A wound that goes through the chest wall will allow air to go inside and the lung will collapse, thus reducing the breathing capacity by half.

Occasionally the blood vessels that run alongside the ribs are cut or torn and bleeding into the chest may occur without any external sign. Should the animal have difficulty in breathing and the chest appear solid on one side, and especially if its lips and gums are pale and there has been the possibility of an accident, the animal should be taken to a vet at once.

CHILL

The term given to the response to a continual cold draught or other temperature-lowering hazards. At one time it was thought to have no real meaning, and that all such responses were due to infection unassociated with chilling. Now it appears that the induced stress can cause symptoms or precipitate latent infection. The animal is dull, with loss of appetite, disinclination to move, and a history of exposure to cold. The animal may recover if warmed up and kept warm, or it may develop an infection such as flu symptoms or even pneumonia.

Horses and donkeys should be rugged up and kept in a snug stable and given a hot bran mash with molasses.

Dogs and cats should be kept in a warm room, small species likewise, or an infra red lamp or bar radiator should be fixed above their cage, care being taken that they don't get too hot.

Budgies respond well to heat – it must be above 72°F (22°C) for best results.

CHOKING

Caused by a foreign body lodged in the throat. The animal may gasp, gulp, paw at its face, or even stop breathing and collapse. Immediately open the animal's mouth (see Restraint), find and remove the cause.

In horses and donkeys it may be a potato or other root vegetable. Hold the animal's mouth open by grasping and pulling out its tongue and dislodge the object. Take care not to push it further back. If unsuccessful after a few minutes, call the vet urgently.

In dogs it is usually a bone, ball, stone or other object of play. Hold the mouth open with the end of a rolling-pin or thick stick, as a gag and hook out the object.

In cats it may also be a needle and thread and often the needle is already swallowed. Hold mouth open by forcing the head back and remove the object with forceps. Take great care when pulling on thread. If there is any difficulty don't delay in consulting the vet. Small animals rarely seem to choke.

COCCIDIA

A single-celled parasite of the intestines. Adults can tolerate it with few, if any, symptoms. But in young animals it can cause diarrhoea that may contain blood.

Different species of animals and birds are affected with separate species of coccidia. There is rarely cross-infection. Rabbits are most commonly affected. Consult your vet for diagnosis and treatment.

COLDS

A name given to a set of symptoms caused by several things. The animal is feverish with elevated body temperature (see Temperature), dullness, poor appetite, and a runny nose (watery or pus-like fluid) and perhaps sneezing.

In the horse and donkey the cause is a respiratory virus against which there are various vaccines (see Vaccines). Isolate the animal to prevent spread of disease, keep it warm but with fresh, dust-free air. Damp hay before feeding to allay dust. There is no specific treatment. If condition gets worse it is probably a secondary infection for which there is treatment, so call the vet. Dogs and cats get their own specific respiratory virus infections. For example, cat flu has several causes and secondary infections. Usually its first cause is either FVR (feline rhinotracheitis virus) or FVC (feline calicivirus). FVR is usually severe, with fever, depression, loss of appetite, nasal and eye discharge, and some ulceration of the mouth. It is very infectious and many die from dehydration. FVC causes the same symptoms but milder. Recovered animals can become carriers.

Rabbits may get myxomatosis from wild rabbits and the early symptoms are flu-like (see Vaccines).

Guinea pigs get a virus pneumonia which is often fatal. There is a treatment which may help if given early in the disease.

Rats and mice get a flu-like disease which can become chronic.

In tortoises, this term is used to describe the condition in which the tortoise is not eating, appears dull, lethargic, and has a nasal discharge and perhaps respiratory problems. There are a variety of causes and for accurate diagnosis and treatment consult your vet. Infections are predisposed by inadequate housing, poor diet, unsuitable environmental temperature, and stress.

COLIC
Is acute pain in the abdomen. In horses and donkeys the cause is usually indigestion due to bad food (musty, fermented) or unusual food (gorging on fallen fruit), sudden over-eating (food store door left open). The animal is restless, looks round at its belly, may sweat. Its stomach may gurgle or be absolutely silent. If severe, the animal may lie down and thrash its legs about. Important to keep the animal walking about, which often relieves the gas. There are other more serious causes, so if it's severe or prolonged call the vet, who can inject and dose the animal, or if necessary operate.

Colic is uncommon is other species of pet. Sudden onset of violent symptoms in the dog can be twist of the stomach, which only immediate surgery can cure.

COLLAPSE
Inability to stand and co-ordinate movement. May be sudden or gradual. May be due to heart disease (see Heart), or poisoning (see Poisons), or slipped disc (see Slipped Disc), or a result of acute and serious diseases such as pneumonia, enteritis, kidney disease, etc. Treatments are described under specific conditions but a vet should always be consulted.

COMA
Unconsciousness with flaccid muscles and a falling body temperature. Causes are: poisoning, such as with weed-killers and insect-pest-killers as well as poisons for killing bird pests; lowered blood sugar due to insulin over-dosage; and raised blood sugar from a disease condition. Prolonged exposure to cold can also cause coma, as can brain damage and some diseases.

For treatment, see specific conditions. Keep the animal warm and dry, lying on its side. Open its mouth and pull its tongue out and call the vet.

CONCUSSION
Loss of consciousness due to injury to the brain. Keep the animal

warm, but not hot, lying on its side. Open its mouth and pull its tongue out. If it doesn't recover in half an hour, consult the vet.

CONGENITAL CONDITIONS
Are those the animal is born with but will not pass on to descendants. Little can be done except supportive therapy if suitable. Inherited conditions – see Hereditary Conditions.

CONJUNCTIVITIS
Is inflammation of the mucous membrane lining the eyelids and covering the third eyelid, and is caused by injury, irritants and infections. Injury may be caused by constant wind (dog with head out of car, horse in damaged horsebox), or a blow or scratch or foreign body (grass husk, dust, thorn). Irritants can be pollen or other substances causing allergic reaction (chemical fumes, dust, smoke). The mucous membrane is red, irritated, causing the animal to rub and paw the eye, and there is a discharge which when severe may stick the eyelids together.

Gently bathe the eye with warm boracic acid solution (½ teaspoon to ½ cup of water) or a proprietary eyewash, 3 or 4 times daily, which should wash out any foreign body. The inflammation will rapidly clear up. If not there may be serious damage, or an embedded foreign body, or infection, and professional help is required.

Some infections are contagious.

CONSTIPATION
Is caused by digestive upset or by obstruction to the passage of faeces by such things as tumours, enlarged prostrate, constriction of the bowel, and conditions causing pain during the passage of faeces.

In a horse a dry diet under certain conditions may be the cause, and the same is true in rabbits and hamsters. In the dog and cat a diet that is highly refined (white bread, biscuits, etc.) or one containing a lot of bony material can cause constipation and painful attempts to pass the hard stool.

The first treatment should be a mild laxative that acts by lubrication, e.g. vegetable oil or medicinal liquid paraffin (not paraffin oil). As the effect is bland, large doses may be given – a cupful to a donkey and a pint to a horse twice daily; a tablespoon to a medium-sized dog (e.g., spaniel) and 1 or 2 teaspoons to a cat; a teaspoon to a rabbit; ¼ teaspoon to a hamster two or three times daily. The diet should be changed if necessary (see Diet). If not relieved in two or three days, or if the animal has a fever or is in pain, or if the faeces are soft but there is a problem in passing stools, consult the vet.

Symptoms of constipation in tortoises are stiff, careful movements of hind legs, reluctance to walk, rear end lower than front and perhaps dragging on the ground, lack of appetite, and no noticeable droppings. It may follow hibernation or be caused by faulty diet – too much roughage – or unripened fibrous food, or by swallowing bedding, or too low an environmental temperature. Treat by reviewing diet and bathing impacted material from cloaca. Check temperature of environment. Give 1ml of medicinal liquid paraffin (mineral oil, *not* paraffin oil) obtainable from the chemist. If no improvement, consult your vet as an X-ray for obstruction may be needed.

Constipation in fish causes lack of appetite and swelling of the belly. It is usually caused by incorrect feeding such as too much dry food. To treat fish, try feeding dry food soaked in liquid paraffin. If this doesn't work give a few drops of liquid paraffin into the mouth by a syringe.

CONTRACEPTION

Is possible in many species, and in theory, in all species once the correct medication has been worked out. At the present time it is available for dogs, cats and pigeons. Consult your vet.

CONVULSIONS

Or fits, uncontrollable spasms of muscles often accompanied by disorientation, most common in the dog and cat. The animal may chomp its jaws, froth at the mouth, its body may stiffen, it may fall and paddle its legs with jerky uncontrolled movements. The fit may last a few minutes and the animal return to near normal and appear dazed.

They are caused by such things as brain disease, e.g. a type of distemper or encephalitis; poisoning with weed killers, strychnine, slug killer or lead; a deficiency of calcium (eclampsia) or sugar in the blood; and certain conditions of the liver and urinary system.

Treatment depends on the cause, which means consulting a vet. Remember they last only two or three minutes. Slide the animal on to a waterproof sheet as it may pass urine and faeces and leave it alone and quiet after removing objects on which it could injure itself. Make notes on the symptoms to help your vet with diagnosis.

COPROPHAGIA

Eating faeces.

This is normal for rabbits and birds. It is an aid to digestion and nutrition. Foals get their normal flora in this way.

It is a trait in puppies, as is a tendency to roll in faeces, which they normally grow out of. Occasionally it can become a habit which can only be broken with patience and attention, for it may become established through boredom.

COUGH

May be caused by infections, irritants, certain heart problems, haemorrhage in the lungs from accidents, inhalation of foreign bodies, and parasites in the trachea or lungs.

Treatment depends on the cause.

In the horse, virus infection and lung worms are probably the most common. Horses and donkeys are sometimes susceptible to dusty feed. It is useful to soak hay and straw in water just before feeding: drain and feed damp. Bedding down with peat reduces dust. Some infections can be vaccinated against (see Vaccines).

The dog, in play, may inhale a foreign body. The cat is more careful. Of all the pets, dogs and cats are the most susceptible to road accidents, and any such chest injuries can result in a cough. In all cases of sudden coughing, consult your vet for diagnosis and treatment.

Rabbits, guinea pigs and hamsters seem to snort rather than cough and this is not common.

CUTS
See Wounds

DANDRUFF
An excessive and noticeable shedding of skin cells. The surface cells of the skin are continually flaking off in the normal animal but the rate is slow and not obvious. Any condition which accelerates this process causes dandruff. It is usually due to a mild inflammation of the skin by bacteria, fungi, mange, parasites, or irritants such as detergents or soap, or an allergy (see Skin). Excessive dosing with iodine will also cause dandruff.

In the dog it is usually due to excessive bathing, or ringworm, or dermodectic mange, or even poor health.

The typical cause in the cat is a type of ringworm (a fungal infection – see Ringworm and Skin).

In the horse it may be ringworm too.

In the smaller pets it can be ringworm or allergy to the cage or box in which they are kept (creosote or other wood preservative).

Treatment depends on the cause and diagnosis requires expert help.

DEAFNESS
Partial loss of hearing. It may be due to blockage of the external ear canal caused by excess wax, inflammatory material, polyps or tumours. It may be congenital. It may be hereditary as in breeds such as cocker spaniels, bull terriers and dalmatians. Some drugs such as streptomycin and salicylates are occasionally responsible.

The danger is that the animal cannot hear traffic noise and does not learn to compensate by looking round. The animal is easily startled, a particular problem in the horse.

There is no treatment for congenital deafness. Other causes should be treated by the vet.

DEATH
Cessation of the functioning of the body as a whole. Bodily processes do not cease to work at the same time. For example, hair and nails continue to grow after respiration and blood circulation

cease.

However, if heartbeat and respiration has stopped for more than two to three minutes death will ensue unless the animal is receiving expert veterinary care.

Nevertheless, if your animal collapses suddenly, the heart should be stimulated and artificial respiration be given by rhythmically squeezing the chest wall every two seconds or so. If the heart does not begin to beat within five minutes further efforts are useless. If the heart is still beating, artificial respiration should continue till normal respiration begins or the vet arrives.

DEHYDRATION

A serious condition in which body fluid is depleted. The characteristic symptom is loss of skin elasticity, i.e. if a skin fold is pulled out and released it does not flop back into position but remains elevated for a second or so and returns to place slowly.

The causes are reduced fluid intake, excessive urine output due to renal disease, continued vomiting, and/or diarrhoea, shock, pyometra (see Pyometra) and intestinal obstruction.

The animal will be weak, its eyes sunken, its mouth dry and its pulse rapid. The abdomen may be distended. Treatment depends on cause and expert veterinary attention is necessary as soon as possible. The vet can give fluids intravenously and treat the primary cause.

For dehydration in tortoises see Emaciation.

DEPRAVED APPETITE

See Coprophagia.

Most animals are careful about what they eat. Occasionally horses will eat abnormal things out of boredom. They will chew at their stable or objects such as plastic articles they may come across.

It is thought that when horses nibble at ivy and the bark of trees, and unusual plants when there is good pasture available, it is a sign there is a deficiency of minerals in their diet. Supplementary minerals can be made available, but minerals should not be added to their concentrates without first seeking expert advice.

DEPRESSION

So far as is known, animals are not prone to psychological depression in the same way as human beings. However, extreme stress or psychological shock can cause the animal to become quiet and less responsive.

The usual causes are elevated body temperature, continual pain, disease and poisoning.

Depression is a symptom of ill health. Look for other symptoms to diagnose the cause.

DERMATITIS

Inflammation of the skin (see Skin).

Inflammation of the skin of tortoises can be caused by injuries, parasites, and bacterial or mycotic infections. Consult the vet for diagnosis and treatment. (See Wounds, Ticks, Mites).

DESTRUCTION

Euthanasia, humane killing of an animal.

The method depends on the species:

Horse shooting with a humane killer is satisfactory if done properly by someone with knowledge and skill, e.g. an RSPCA inspector. A shotgun should not be used and it is unlikely that a humane killer or revolver will be available without the trained owner. An alternative humane method is injection of an overdose of anaesthetic intravenously. This can therefore only be done by a vet.

Dog the best method is intravenous barbiturates. Shooting is humane but unsightly.

Cat intravenous barbiturates or chloroform.

Small pets and birds chloroform.

Fish tricaine or ether in the water.

These drugs are only available to a veterinary surgeon, to whom the animal should be taken.

DEW CLAWS

Are extra claws (a fifth toe) that sometimes occur on the back feet, and often on the front feet.

Because they can get caught on things and injured it is better to have them surgically removed. The best time is soon after birth when they can be snipped off with scissors. Later the operation is more complicated. The advice and help of a vet should be sought.

DIABETES

Is of two types – Mellitus and Insipidus.

Diabetes Mellitus is due to damage of certain cells in the pancreas due to inflammation, or damage, or cancer, and it may have no known cause, but can be made worse by dosing with oestrogens and corticosteroids (cortisones). Symptoms are increased thirst, appetite and urine production, accompanied by loss of weight. The animal is depressed and dehydrated. Later it may vomit and develop cataracts of the eyes. Diabetes Mellitus affects dogs and cats and is not normally diagnosed in other pets. Treatment with insulin is used, together with special diet. A vet must be consulted.

Diabetes Insipidus is caused by a lack of a circulatory hormone called ADH, or failure of the kidneys to respond to the hormone. The animal drinks excessively and passes a lot of urine, and has to be distinguished from a case of chronic nephritis. Special tests are required to test for this condition and measure its severity. Treatment is not very satisfactory.

DIARRHOEA

Can be caused by a sudden change of diet or bad or damaged food, various infections, allergic conditions, parasites, poisoning, cancer, and some diseases of unknown cause. The animal passes loose or watery faeces that often have a bad odour and an abnormal colour, with increased frequency.

The animal may or may not be eating, and it may or may not have a temperature depending on the cause.

If the animal still has an appetite and a normal temperature, and is not too depressed, the cause is probably dietary. Withhold food but supply water and observe carefully. Usually once the offending material has been got rid of the diarrhoea will stop. This takes one or two days and the animal can then be given low-protein food. If it is a herbivore give fresh hay and low-protein concentrates. If a carnivore give carbohydrates (rice, brown bread, potatoes) flavoured with gravy – but no red meat for several days and then gradually return the diet to normal.

If the animal is depressed and has an elevated temperature and has no appetite, expert help should be sought for it may have a specific disease like distemper, parvo, canine hepatitis, feline enteritis, or a bacterial or viral infection of the intestines.

If the diarrhoea is prolonged, or if it comes and goes without apparent cause, again seek veterinary help for it may be caused by an allergy to an item of diet, or a cancer or a more unusual disease condition.

If the onset is sudden and the animal appears very ill and depressed, with, possibly, vomiting and blood in the faeces, poisoning should be suspected and veterinary assistance sought immediately.

Unless the condition is mild and the animal seems otherwise normal, it is not wise to dose with any medicine. However, if the condition is mild and the animal appears to be in good spirits, but the diarrhoea doesn't cease in one or two days, medicine can be given. There are many kinds on the market, and the best is a mixture containing substances which protect the injured lining of the intestines, such as kaolin, pectin, magnesium carbonate, and powdered charcoal. Bismuth compounds are particularly soothing to inflamed mucous membranes.

Morphine mixtures are sometimes used to stop diarrhoea. Morphine acts by slowing down movements of the intestines. The danger is that it may cause constipation. It is important to make sure that the animal has all the drinking water it wants, as it can become dehydrated – which is more serious.

DIET

The purpose of a diet is to provide the body's building and replacement materials, and supply energy to allow the body to function. A secondary requisite is to keep the digestive system working harmoniously. Problems are caused by imbalance making the animal put on weight or become too thin, and also causing various metabolic problems exhibited as ill health. Ill health can also be caused by deficiencies of essential elements such as certain minerals and vitamins.

Problems are also caused by food that is bad or decomposed or contaminated or containing poisons, or by irregular feeding, or by rapid changes in the food constituents.

The basic elements are protein, carbohydrates, fat, fibre and minerals, including trace elements and vitamins. Requirements differ with each species.

Horses and donkeys require a mixture of roughage (hay, grass, and their equivalents) and concentrates (grain mixtures, loose or pressed into nuts or pellets). The relative amounts of these depend on the condition and size of the animal and the work it is doing. A fat horse or donkey, idle in a field or box, will require little or no concentrate. A thin but idle animal will require more and an animal that is worked hard daily will require a lot.

It is essential that the hay is good and undamaged, and that the concentrate mixture is balanced for minerals and contains enough protein (which varies greatly from cereal to cereal) and trace minerals and vitamins. An animal will require more vitamins in the food if it cannot graze on a pasture for most of the grazing period. It is important to feed the best hay available, the ready-made concentrate mixture or nuts that are guaranteed to be balanced and complete are the best way to buy and feed concentrates. Mixing your own is not for the inexperienced amateur.

The hay to concentrate ratio is approximately as follows, depending on condition of the animal:

	Hay	Grain	
Foal	50:	50	by weight
Adult resting	100:	0	by weight
Adult mod. work	50:	50	by weight
Mare pregnant	70:	30	by weight
Mare lactating:			
(at first)	40:	60	by weight
(then)	60:	40	by weight

The amount of hay and concentrates is approximately 2 kg. per 100 kg. body weight per day divided into two feeds (4½ lb. per 220 lb). The amount of concentrate required when the animal is grazing pasture will depend on the nutritional value of the pasture. In spring and early summer little or no concentrate will be required unless the animal is losing condition (check for worms – see Parasites). In late summer and autumn concentrates will be required, for the nutritional value of the grazing is low.

Extra care is necessary when animals are grazing rich pasture (see Laminitis).

Foals require highly digestible food – e.g. feed containing 20% digestible protein at a rate of ½ kilo per day at 2 months of age for a hunter foal – less for a donkey foal.

It is important to feed the same mixture for changes may cause indigestion. Most animals do not like a rapid change of food. Boredom with the diet is certainly not a problem. And try to feed at the same times each day, and not immediately after exercise. Fresh water should always be available. However, if an animal has been working very hard and lost a lot of sweat it is unwise to let it drink its fill of cold water. Good feeding practices and sound nutrition are the basis of health.

Dogs It is a fallacy to think that because they are carnivores they should be fed nothing but meat. A totally meat diet will cause nothing but problems. Once you know what the dog likes and know that it is nutritionally suitable, don't make radical changes because you feel it must get bored with the same old diet. Changes could upset the animal. In the wild, carnivore species eat vegetable material directly, and more often than not the bowel contents of their prey contain vegetable matter as well as hair and feathers which provide bulk to the diet.

The dog's diet must contain certain vegetable material to help provide energy and supply fibre as bulk. It should have a high protein content for the young growing animal, and much less for the adult and ageing dog. It must contain adequate minerals (more are required by the growing animal) and vitamins. The simplest way to feed your dog is with the ready-made and balanced diets (either canned or dried) prepared by reputable pet-food manufacturers.

Remember, don't upset the nutritional balance by feeding other items unless as titbits in small amounts. Consult the manufacturer before adding minerals and vitamins to the diet.

Alternatively, a diet can be made up in the home as follows:

Puppies 6 weeks–3 months require a lot of high-energy food in relation to protein, in a ratio of 1:1 (bitches' milk contains 40% fat and 35% protein approximately). This can be provided with a mixture such as:

Wholemeal bread or Weetabix 1 part by weight

Cooked meat (inc. liver and offal) 2 parts by weight

Milk 5 parts by weight

Vitamins – as per manufacturer's instructions

Mineral mix as per manufacturer's instructions

Total daily requirements per pound (0.45 kg.) body weight is twice that of an adult per pound body weight. Give this mixture in four feeds, as much as the pup can eat in 15 minutes and then take away what is left over.

Puppies 3 months–1 year Increase the wholemeal bread or biscuit until it equals the meat in weight and begin to add cooked vegetables (carrots and cabbage are best) to give more bulk and fibre, increasing to up to one-sixth of whole mix at one year old. Feed three times a day, reducing to twice a day, as much as the animal can eat in 15 minutes.

Adult dogs The lean meat should be reduced to 4 oz. (113 g.) per day for each 15 lb. (6.80 kg.) of body weight and the rest of the diet increased to an amount the animal will readily eat and remain in good condition (not too thin, or – which is more likely – not too fat). This depends on the dog's own metabolism and the exercise it takes. Brown rice may be given at times and cheese can replace some meat. Vegetables must be given to provide fibre. Mix them thoroughly with diet and the diet can be flavoured with gravy.

Puppies and adults benefit from having a large, fresh, uncooked cow bone or joint to chew upon. Do not feed cooked bones as they are inclined to splinter (especially poultry, sheep and pig). A mineral mix and vitamin supplement may be added to the diet according to the manufacturer's instructions.

Always have fresh drinking water available.

Cats The cat is more discriminating about what it eats and hates a change of diet. A good commercial cat food will contain all that the animal requires and can be fed twice daily in amounts that the animal will decide. Occasionally a cat may become greedy and get too fat and so its diet should be restricted. To make up a diet, follow the instructions as for dogs above. Milk is given separately and cooked meat and wholemeal bread or its equivalent, and a small amount of cooked vegetable, ground and mixed into a hamburger with enough juice to make it moist. Alternatively, the mixture can be cooked with the meat to produce a tinned-food-like product.

If cats are fed fish and meat separately they will not eat vegetable material and will not get a balanced diet. Dermatitis and other problems may result.

Small pets Small mammals such as rabbits, hamsters, guinea pigs, rats and mice are all vegetarians. They must be given good hay for roughage, otherwise they may eat their bedding, and a concentrate mixture of cereals. The pet shop will provide a balanced mixture, which must be available all the time. These small pets rarely eat too much if it is always available. Fresh water should also be available always. Remember, do not change the diet suddenly. If you decide to give them fresh green food, then introduce a little at first and gradually increase it. And make sure it is thoroughly washed.

Birds Budgies, canaries and pigeons should be fed the grain mixture prepared and sold by reputable manufacturers. It is essential to provide grit (also available from bird food retailers) which is used by the bird in its gizzard to grind the food.

Birds require vitamin B12 which some species obtain by eating their own droppings that are a few days old, which allows bacterial action to produce the vitamin. Otherwise it must be added to the diet. Titbits like green food may be given, care being taken to wash it thoroughly.

Tortoises are omnivores. They eat earthworms, insects and carrion as well as plants. It is necessary to give a varied diet to supply minerals and vitamins as well as protein. Leafy plants on their own are not enough, though they obtain much of their fluid requirement in that way. They eat fruit, dandelions, clover, grass, lettuce and other leaves. Give finely chopped liver, sliced boiled eggs, earthworms and snails to form 10 per cent of the total diet – not more.

Do *not* feed milk, bread, cheese, sausages, minced beef nor the leaves of rhubarb and beetroot (which are poisonous). Avoid plants contaminated with pesticides.

In the winter supplement the diet with minerals and vitamins specially prepared for animals such as Vionate (Squibb & Co) available from your vet. This product is particularly good for hatchlings.

Fish Tropical fish and certain cold-water fish have special dietary requirements and specialist advice should be sought. Goldfish and many cold-water fish normally eat far more in the summer months than in winter. Goldfish can do without food for weeks, and it is best to get a neighbour to feed them whilst you are on holiday as overfeeding can be a hazard by polluting the water.

Fresh or dried food obtained from a specialist shop may be given and vegetable material may be added as a supplement for carp and barbs.

The biggest danger is overfeeding. If the fish are hungry they will rush around and eat quickly. If they don't, give them less. Fish have small stomachs.

Fresh food are earthworms, whiteworms, daphnia and fresh meat or liver from the butcher.

Dried foods are biscuit meal, dried meat, egg or insects. Soften them before feeding. Avoid mixes with too much vegetable material as if it is not eaten it pollutes the water. Cooked lettuce, spinach or cabbage can be tried.

Be careful of the source of water plants as they can carry disease.

Feed at one part of the tank so that if a lot is not eaten it can be removed.

DISEASE
Any departure from health caused by disfunction of organs or

systems brought about by infections, cancers, or other unknown causes.

It is usually, but not always, predisposed by stress which may be psychological or physical. The layman usually assumes disease to be caused by invasion of the body by a micro-organism. However, some diseases such as diabetes or urinary calculi are not infections.

Diseases are diagnosed by first recognising a pattern of symptoms, and then making the necessary laboratory examinations to find the infective agent or the biochemical changes.

Most, if not all, infections cause the animal to be dull with poor appetite and an elevated body temperature, at least at the beginning. Most affect one or two organs whose malfunction causes more specific symptoms such as coughing or diarrhoea or blood in urine, etc. A raised body temperature is one of the body's methods of dealing with the infection. Loss of appetite is another for it saves the complication of trying to deal with food. Keep the animal protected from draughts and getting cold. Provide clean water and consult your vet.

Tortoises are prone to infection caused by bacteria, viruses, protozoa and fungi. The general symptoms are loss of appetite and weight, weakness, and one or more of the following: discharge from eyes, nose, mouth; bad breath; noisy breathing; vomiting; diarrhoea; blood in mouth or in diarrhoea. To make an accurate diagnosis and treatment consult an expert (see Mouth, Eyes, Nose, Diarrhoea, Breathing).

Disease in fish is caused through stress, tank problems, faulty feeding, and introduced infections. Many diseases affect the surface of the fish (see Skin). There are a number of parasites, internal as well as external, which cause disease. Symptoms apart from visible lesions are poor appetite, loss of weight, sluggishness, circling and loss of balance. (See under specific names.) It is advisable to remove and isolate diseased fish from the tank to prevent spread of infection.

DISINFECTANT

A substance used to kill germs.

Phenol (carbolic) type disinfectants can be dangerous to cats and dogs. There is a Ministry of Agriculture approved list of disinfectants for farm animals. Some have distinct odours and others have little or no smell.

In recent years some very effective disinfectants have been discovered. One of the best and safest is an iodophor which is based on iodine. When it loses its potency the beer colour (the strength at which it is used) goes clear. With other disinfectants, the odour may remain whilst the power has disappeared.

Disinfectants should always be used in the strength recommended by the manufacturer. If too dilute they may not work, and if too strong, they may injure the animal and they are no more effective – indeed some are less effective.

The best and safest for tortoises is iodophor in a weak beer-coloured solution.

For fish tanks and equipment the same disinfectants are effective, but great care must be taken to rinse out all traces of the disinfectant with clean water before they are used for fish. As some fish infections are fairly resistant to disinfectants, overnight soaking is recommended.

DISLOCATION
Describes a joint that is out of place.

The animal will probably be in pain and if a limb is affected, it will be lame. Consult your vet as soon as possible. Many cases require an anaesthetic followed by an X-ray and replacement to normal, and usually bandaging to hold the joint in place. The earlier they are treated the better, and there is every chance of a return to normal unless there is a fracture as well.

If a bird's wing is dislocated and there is no fracture, there is every chance it will fly again.

DOSING
Whether the medicine is solid or liquid, animals resent being dosed because the medicine has a strange taste and the procedure is new. Manufacturers sometimes try to disguise the taste, or even add an attractive taste, to make dosing easier. But that is not much help if the animal has lost its appetite.

Dosing a horse with creamy medicine

Horses and donkeys, because of their size and strength, are difficult to dose. Treatment for worms is by far the most frequent remedy given by mouth nowadays. Dosing has been made easier since manufacturers produced the medicine in the form of a cream packed in a plastic syringe, which is poked into the side of the mouth and the cream squeezed out along the molar teeth. The size of horses' digestive system and the fermentation that takes place interferes with many drugs, so it is usual to give antibiotics by injection which ensures a therapeutic level with a much smaller dose. Pills are rarely given, and liquids only occasionally – usually by the vet using a tube passed up the nostril and into the stomach, which avoids the danger of the animal choking and getting the liquid into its lungs.

Smaller animals, however, are often dosed with pills and liquids.

Dogs are dosed with liquids by holding the animal's mouth closed and the head pointing upwards, and then inserting a finger into the corner of the dog's lips and hooking out the cheek pouch, into which a helper can pour the liquid. Keep the dog's mouth closed and head up, and massage the throat region to make the animal swallow as the liquid drains between the teeth into the mouth.

It is more of a struggle with short-nosed dogs to hold the mouth closed and the head up. A plastic syringe is a great help here, for it can be poked into the much smaller cheek pouch of these breeds.

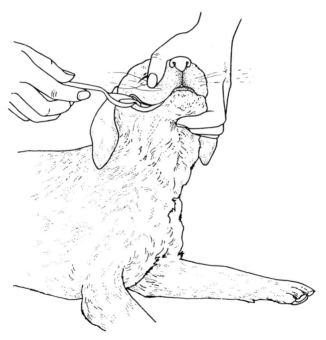

Dosing a dog with liquid medicine

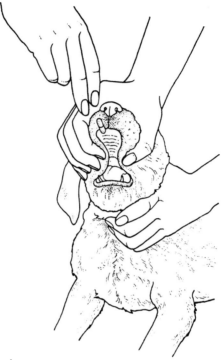

Giving a pill to a dog

To give a dog a pill or tablet, hold its head and its mouth open. (It helps to push the lips in between the animal's molars, which keeps the mouth open and prevents fingers being bitten.) A helper can now place the tablet on the back of the tongue where it is thickest. Release the dog's jaws and massage the throat: the dog can then only avoid swallowing the pill if it was not placed far enough back.

Cats are more difficult. The basic technique is the same as for dogs, but it is safer to use a small plastic syringe for liquids, and to put the pill on the cat's tongue with a small teaspoon, or better still, tweezers, so as to avoid being bitten. Give liquid in small amounts, to avoid it accidentally going down the windpipe. If the animal coughs or chokes lower its head at once.

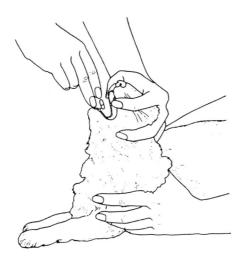

Giving a pill to a cat

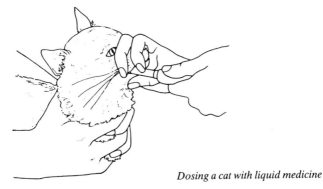

Dosing a cat with liquid medicine

Rabbits may be dosed in the same way as dogs and cats. Smaller pets are more difficult simply because of their size.

Liquid paraffin is often used for constipation, and because of its blandness most animals will take it in the food or floated on drinking water or milk, thus avoiding the problems of dosing.

Tortoises are better injected when that is possible, for their digestive processes are so slow that the drug is not absorbed fast enough. Many medicines are acceptable to them when mixed with food, as foul tastes are not a problem.

DRINKING

Fresh clean water should always be available.

If the animal is drinking more than normal for no apparent reason such as excessively hot weather, and it seems to be out of sorts, it may be wise to consult your vet.

If the animal is drinking less than normal and it is dull, then consult your vet.

Small mammals don't drink much, but they do need some water, so always make it available.

DROWNING

Animals, particularly horses and dogs, can swim fairly well. Cats can swim but less strongly. They can remain afloat and breathing for a time. Soon they inhale water and lose consciousness. Danger sites are rivers and quarries with high straight sides preventing the animal from clambering out. Ornamental ponds and swimming pools, especially half-empty ones, are dangerous. Animals fall in and drown when ice over a pond or lake gives way with their weight. Dogs have drowned when trying to swim in a rough sea.

To save an animal, tie a rope or twine to anything that will float and throw it to the animal to cling to while you pull it towards the bank.

If the animal is unconscious and its heart is still beating, lay it on its side with its head sloping downwards from tail to head so that water can run out of its lungs. Then rhythmically and steadily give artifical respiration, using the flat of your hands to press on the chest and then release about 15 or 20 times per minute. Continue until breathing recommences. As long as the heart is beating there is every hope you may be successful.

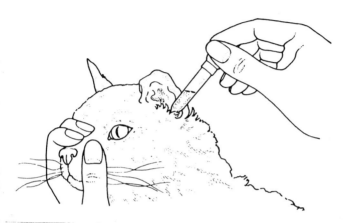

Putting drops in a cat's ear

EAR
Lobe Swelling of the lobe is not uncommon in dogs, and can affect cats. It is usually due to a burst blood vessel under the skin, causing a blood blister or haematoma. The cause is injury, either self-inflicted by scratching the ear vigorously, or shaking the head and banging the ear lobe on a solid object. Or it may result from a bite from another dog.

If it is small it will gradually be absorbed and leave the ear lobe slightly thicker than normal. However, there is always the risk that another injury may cause it to get bigger. The best treatment is an operation by a vet.

If the ear lobe is injured and bleeding externally, the animal usually shakes its head and showers blood everywhere and it looks as if it has lost a lot of blood. There is scarcely any danger of the animal bleeding to death. (See Haemorrhage for symptoms).

Unless the wound is large and suturing is necessary, dressing and bandaging is all that is needed (see Wounds).

Canal ends at the ear drum and nature has lined it with cells that produce wax, and some hair, the purpose of which is to protect the canal. Some animals produce more wax than normal and from time to time it has to be cleaned out. This can be done gently with ear swabs, provided there is no inflammation.

The canal can become infested with a small mite like a miniature spider which is passed from one animal to another. This stimulates the production of wax which is dark and causes irritation. The animal will shake its head, rub the ear on the floor, and scratch vigorously with its paw.

The canal can become infected with bacteria causing severe inflammation and pain and a discharge of pus. Occasionally irritation and pain occur suddenly. The animal holds its head to one side with the sore ear down. This could be caused by a grass seed or some such foreign body going down the ear canal.

In all of these cases professional help is required to examine, diagnose and treat with the correct medicament (see also Deafness).

Tortoises can hear, though the ear is not well developed. The inner ear, which is concerned with maintenance of balance, is well developed. The ear drum is level with the skin so there is no ear canal. Otitis media (middle ear disease) causes a swelling of the ear drum and needs lancing to remove the cheesy plug of wax.

ECLAMPSIA

A type of fit or tetany that occurs occasionally in animals just after giving birth. It is due to a lack of circulating calcium in the blood.

The animal is first restless, then begins to pant and appears nervous. Later it becomes stiffer with muscular spasms, and if the case is severe, and not treated immediately with an injection of calcium, the bitch or queen may collapse and die. Call your vet at once. Treatment is usually followed by a rapid recovery. There are other causes of fits (see Fits) with which it may be confused.

ECZEMA

The name given to an area of inflamed, weeping or encrusted and oozing skin. A type of dermatitis, caused by infections with bacteria, mange or ringworm, or due to hypersensitivity of the skin, or damage caused by irritant substances.

Treatment depends on the cause, and expert help is needed (see Mange, Ringworm and Skin).

EGGBOUND

Describes the condition when a bird is unable to lay a fully developed egg, which becomes lodged in the passage making it impossible or difficult for the bird to pass droppings normally, and thus causes it to become dull and off its food.

The cloaca will be swollen and probably inflamed, and the lower abdomen swollen. The egg may or may not be seen inside. A hot, humid environment will help. If not, try dropping olive oil into the cloaca and gently massaging the area. Take care not to break the egg, or more serious inflammation will result from the sharp pieces of shell. If not successful, seek expert help.

Sometimes the egg breaks inside the passage and the area becomes swollen and possibly infected. Early professional help is necessary or the bird will soon die.

EGGS

Tortoises can lay between 1 and 15 eggs in a clutch. They are slightly oval and white in colour (see Breeding).

Occasionally the tortoise cannot lay the egg (eggbinding). The animal may appear to be searching for something and refuse to feed. It may start to dig holes. If placed in deep water it is heavy enough to sink (remove at once or it may drown). Eggbinding is caused by an imbalance of calcium and phosphorous in the diet, in most cases. Too much calcium causes excess shell growth which is lumpy.

If the egg is not passed within a week, take the animal to the vet.

ELECTRIC SHOCK

From 220 volts can be lethal to animals, particularly small animals, but also to horses and donkeys. They do not have the resistance to this voltage that humans have. Death is caused by heart failure. It results when the animal bites through the insulation of wire carrying the current. Usually the muscular spasms throw the animal clear of the wire. But it is wise to turn off the electricity before touching the animal.

Lay the animal flat and apply pressure over the chest and heart with the flat of your hand and immediately release and repeat about 20 times per minute. This will provide artificial respiration and massage the heart and provide some circulation of the blood. Call the vet urgently. He can inject heart stimulant if it doesn't start to beat from massage. There may be some burning of tissue by the current so treat for burns.

ELIZABETHAN COLLAR

A wide collar made of stiff cardboard or plastic that stands out from the neck like a ruff, and is used to stop the animal scratching its ears or head region.

EMACIATION

Extreme loss of weight caused by many diseases such as infections, cancers, parasites, intestinal and renal disorders, and diabetes.

Professional help is necessary to diagnose the cause.

Loss of weight in tortoises can be caused by incorrect diet, parasites, disease and hibernation (see Diet, Parasites, Enteritis, Hibernation).

It may also be caused by dehydration due to lack of drinking water, either because it is not available, or because it is in a container with high sides so that the tortoise can't reach it. Or the environmental temperature may be too *low* so that the tortoise is not active enough to drink.

Treat for dehydration by bathing the animal for ten minutes three times per day in clean water that has been boiled and allowed to cool to 75°F (24°C). After the first one or two bathings the tortoise should drink. If it does not, it is necessary to give water by mouth, e.g. by syringe, slowly with great care. Give a good diet (see Diet).

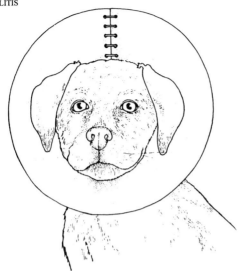

An Elizabethan collar on a dog

EMETICS
Substances which cause vomiting and are used to get the animal to sick up poisons (see Vomiting).

ENCEPHALITIS
Inflammation of the substance of the brain. It can produce a variety of symptoms depending on the part of the brain affected. In foreign countries a common cause is rabies (Britain is free due to our strict quarantine laws).

Symptoms of encephalitis caused by other infections may include dullness, abnormal behaviour, staggering and falling down, and possibly a rise in body temperature.

Always seek professional help as soon as possible.

ENDOMETRITIS
Inflammation of the uterus (see Metritis).

ENTERITIS

Inflammation of the bowels (see Diarrhoea), and is caused by infection with viruses or bacteria, or by infestation with worms or coccidia, or is produced by poisons, or is an allergic response.

It causes pain and diarrhoea. Unless it is mild, professional help should be sought for accurate diagnosis and treatment.

Inflammation of the bowel in tortoises can be caused by wrong food which decomposes. For example bread and milk, or rotting food, or food contaminated with pesticides. Bacterial, protozoal and mycotic infections all cause enteritis which causes diarrhoea. Consult your vet for diagnosis and treatment.

In fish the main symptom is bloody or yellowish-coloured, slimy excrement. Immediately fast the fish for four or five days at least and change the food.

EPILEPSY

Collapse, loss of consciousness and convulsions, and the cause is not known. (See also Poisons, Rabies and Eclampsia).

EXERCISE

Species vary in their need for exercise. Horses and dogs require regular exercise to remain fit and healthy. Small animals are continually active, and if given enough space will exercise themselves.

Cats don't seem to require exercise beyond a type of callisthenics they do themselves to remain fit.

Horses should be given light exercise – a few miles walking per day at first – and then gradually increase the speed and distance. Horses that are kept in a fairly large paddock will exercise themselves. However, they will require training before they are fit for a lot of work.

Dogs need to be able to run about and use their noses to sniff out other animals otherwise they become bored and stressed. It is the change of scenery from their own home and garden as much as the exercise, that is necessary.

Though it is common to keep budgies and canaries in small cages, and they seem to adapt well enough, it is better to have an aviary in

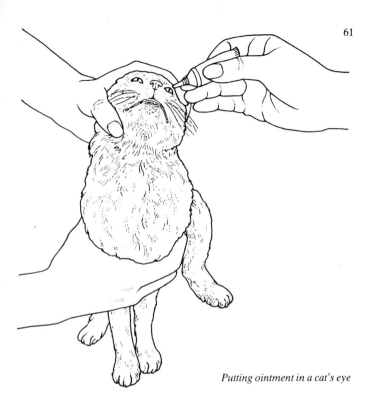

Putting ointment in a cat's eye

which they can fly, or allow them to fly in the house at least once per day.

EYE

Discharge of pus-like material is a sign of inflammation of the surface of the eyelids or conjunctivitis (see Conjunctivitis).
The Third Eyelid is an extra flap inside the eyelids in the corner nearest the nose. Its purpose is to aid in sweeping foreign material from the surface of the eye. Sometimes, especially in cats, it may be seen one-third or half-way across the eyeball and gives the animal a strange appearance, for it usually affects both eyes. It is not

dangerous except as a sign that the animal may be in poor health and depressed or suffering from upper respiratory disease. Unless the animal is ill, don't worry, it will go away. It may be associated with conjunctivitis.

Entropian Some animals are born with, or soon develop, inturning eyelids. Usually only a few eyelashes are folded inwards so that they scrape on the surface of the eyeball and cause a pus-like discharge. The only cure is an operation, which is usually successful.

Keratitis is an inflammation of the surface of the eyeball. Causes are similar to those causing conjunctivitis. In addition a thorn or sharp point scratching the surface of the eyeball can cause it. It is quite painful and the normally clear eyeball becomes cloudy or milky white. If both eyes are affected it may be due to disease. It is important to consult your vet at once. There are other diseases it could be and an accurate diagnosis is needed.

If keratitis is left too long without treatment an ulcer may form which is more difficult to treat, and there is the possibility it may burst and release the fluid in the anterior chamber of the eye, and sight could be lost.

Cataract is opacity of the lens. The surface of the eyeball is still clear and the pupil appears cloudy. It may affect one or both eyes and can occur at any age. It can be hereditary or accompany inherited retinal disease. It can accompany glaucoma, or diabetes mellitus, or be caused by toxins or injury. Once it has settled down (there is no treatment for the cataract itself), and the accompanying disease (if any) has been dealt with, and if the sight is badly affected, your vet can operate and remove the lens and allow some vision.

Swelling of the eyeball is called glaucoma, and is due to faulty drainage of the eye fluids or to dislocation of the lens, or to haemorrhage or tumours inside the eyeball. You must consult your vet.

Horner's Syndrome is damage to part of the nerve supply to the eye from injury or cancer, or inflammation of the ear. The affected pupil is dilated, the eyelids drooping, and the third eyelid is protruding. Again you must consult your vet regarding these symptoms.

Blindness can be caused by changes in the eyeball such as keratitis, cataract, or damage to the lens and damage to the retina from inflammation or detachment, or separation of the retina. Damage of the optic nerve is another cause, as are certain types of disease of the brain. Blindness can also be caused by certain diseases such as toxoplasmosis and diabetes mellitus, and by some poisons.

In all cases blindness is noticed when the animal bumps into objects. It is of particular concern in the horse and donkey and less important in smaller animals, which seem to be able to adapt fairly well.

It is essential to consult your vet.

There is a scheme set up by the British Veterinary Association, the Kennel Club, and the International Sheepdog Society to examine breeding dogs for inheritable eye disease and give a certificate to each animal that is free. Thus it is possible to be sure that the puppy you purchase is free from hereditary eye disease.

The most common eye problem in tortoises is swelling of the eyelids and discharge due to a vitamin A deficiency. Bacterial infection does not cause swelling of the eyelids. Mycotic infection may affect the glands that lubricate the eye. The eyelids often get stuck together in all the above conditions. For treatment, first look at the diet and correct any deficiencies, give Vitamin A (carrot juice or Vionate). Bacterial infection is treated with eye ointment.

If one eye is affected it may be an injury due to sharp objects in the accommodation, such as straw, twigs or wire. Bathe the eye with boracic solution – one teaspoonful in a small cup of warm, boiled water. If it doesn't improve, consult the vet.

If the eyes are discharging and possibly closed, and there is a nasal discharge as well and respiratory problems, and the animal refuses to feed properly there may be an irritant in the bedding, either dust or ammonia or some other irritant. If not, the cause must be an infection. Consult your vet.

In fish, opacity of the eye may be due to tuberculosis or a parasite, and swelling or protrusion of the eye is caused by tuberculosis parasites and kidney disease. Fungus can affect the eye and is visible as white or grey-white threads resembling cotton wool. It usually follows injury.

Treatment is to touch the fungus with a match or small brush dipped in 1% or 2% silver nitrate solution in *distilled water*, followed by touching the eye with a 1% solution of potassium dichromate to neutralise the silver nitrate.

FAECES

The amount, consistency, colour and odour of the faeces can tell us a lot about the well-being of the animal.

Horse faeces are formed into fairly uniform-sized balls of a greenish brown colour, and with a not unpleasant odour. The balls, of roughly tennis-ball size, are formed by the pockets in the large bowel where some digestion and a lot of absorption takes place. If the faeces become:

a)   too dry, it may be the diet is too astringent, or the horse is running a temperature.

b)   Too loose, the horse may be feeding on rich young grass, or it may have enteritis or worms.

c)   dark brown or black in colour, there may be bleeding into the intestines.

d)   bad-smelling, there is a digestive upset.

Dog faeces are sausage-shaped, brown in colour (though this will vary with the diet), and with a strong odour that is not pleasant. If the faeces become:

a)   too dry, the diet is wrong – perhaps too many bones, or the animal may have a temperature.

b)   too loose, it usually means the bowels are inflamed.

c)   the colour can vary but if it becomes white it means the dog is getting too many bones.

d)   bad-smelling means it has indigestion, perhaps from eating something unusual, or it has inflammation of the bowel.

Cats are secretive animals; they pass sausage-shaped faeces of putty-like consistency, and any deviation is abnormal.

Small mammals like rabbits, hamsters, guinea pigs, rats and mice all pass brown pelleted faeces that have very little odour. Any deviation from this is abnormal.

Birds don't pass urine. The end product from the kidney filtration is mixed with the faeces and they are passed together – the whitish element is from the urinary system. The excreta have little odour when fresh, and are an olive to greenish colour depending on the diet. Loose, bright green faeces mean there is trouble and the birds should be observed closely, and if other symptoms such as lack of appetite arise consult your vet.

Faeces of fish are normally formed and solid.

FAINTING

Sudden loss of consciousness is not common in healthy animals. It can occur in some diseases, particularly heart disease. (See also Shock, Convulsions, Fits).

FAT

Over-fat and overweight animals are more prone to some diseases. It is caused by overfeeding and under-exercising and possibly an unbalanced diet (see Diet).

FEATHER or FUR PICKING

and the loss of feathers or fur are caused by boredom leading to self-mutilation or by disease. Birds such as those of the parrot type which are flock birds, and strong fliers, and are often kept in solitary confinement in small cages, are most prone to develop the habit of feather picking. Some may even pick themselves bald.

Horses may sometimes bite each other's manes and dogs sometimes mutilate their tails.

Cats and small mammals rarely indulge in this habit.

Loss of feathers or fur (hair) can be caused by several infections such as ringworm and mange, and by external parasites such as lice, fleas and mites.

It is necessary to consult your vet for an exact diagnosis.

FEEDING

See Diet.

Tortoises will eat nearly every day provided they are in their normal environmental temperature range. It is important to remove all uneaten food every day, as decomposing food may cause problems.

FEET

Next to diet, the most important thing to pay attention to is the well-being of the feet of your horse or donkey. The hooves grow continuously and have to be trimmed regularly, even if the animal has no shoes, for otherwise the horn of the hoof may crack or split.

When the animal is shod it is essential to clean out the sole of each foot each day, and make sure the animal has a reasonable dry surface to stand on, otherwise the sole becomes soft, and bacteria can penetrate and cause necrosis.

The shoes must be removed every four to six weeks and the wall cut back, and the animal re-shod, otherwise the shoe is pushed forward, and the heel of the shoe can bruise the sole.

Make sure there are no loose nails as these can puncture through to the sensitive tissue. The shoeing must be done by an expert otherwise the whole alignment of the limb joints is affected, which can cause lameness.

Aeration is important for the health of the horn, and overfeeding can result in laminitis (see Laminitis).

The nails of dogs and sometimes cats can become too long and must be cut. Take care not to injure the sensitive tissue in the centre of the nail. It is well supplied with blood and can bleed profusely. If this happens, swab with strong iodine to stop the haemorrhage.

The pads are fairly tough, but occasionally, especially in larger dogs, the pad can be penetrated by a thorn, or cut. The animal will be lame. If the cut is large or you cannot get the thorn out, take it to a vet. Otherwise, for a small cut, the foot can be cleaned and bandaged (see Wounds and Bandaging).

Dew claws are digits that are found on the fore limbs, and not infrequently on the hind limbs, of dogs. Sometimes they are firmly jointed like a normal digit, often they are hanging loose. Because they can catch on carpets and such-like, and get wrenched and torn, it is common practice to remove them when the puppy is a few days old. Usually they can be snipped off with sharp scissors. Because they bleed profusely and a local anaesthetic is required, it is better to get the vet to do it. Later in life the operation may require a general anaesthetic. Consult your vet.

Not infrequently the nails of budgies and canaries grow too long and have to be cut. Otherwise they catch on the perch and the toe is wrenched or even dislocated.

FEVER
The term given to a rise in body temperature caused by an infection. The normal body temperatures are:

Horse	38°C	(100.5°F)
Donkey	38.2°C	(100.8°F)
Dog	38.5°C	(101°F)
Cat	38.5°C	(101°F)
Rabbit	39.5°C	(104°F)
Hamster	39.4°C	(103°F)
Guinea Pig	39.0°C	(103.5°F)
Bird (depending on species)	39.5°C – 42.5°C	
	(104°F – 108°F)	

These figures are average and a range of plus or minus 0.5 is normal.

FILTRATION
Of fish tanks is not essential. Its purpose is to remove particles of suspended waste matter and some toxic substances. There are two main types, the external box filter and the under-gravel filter, which is placed in the bottom of the tank. In both, water is drawn from the tank and passed through layers of glass wool, activated charcoal and stones in that order before returning clean to the tank. Filters eventually become dirty and have to be cleaned and the activated charcoal replaced.

FINS
Of fish are susceptible to injury and disease due to parasites and bacteria. Excessive acidity or alkalinity of the water may cause the fins to fray.

Fin rot is caused by a bacterium and the treatment is to place the fish in a solution of 10ml of 1% solution of phenoxythol (2 phenoxyethanol) in 1 litre of water.

Sulphadiazine and chloramphenicol are also effective and treatment may be obtained from the vet.

A fungus called Ichthyosporidium hoferi can attack the fins but normally affects the internal organs.

It is one of the most common diseases and there is no specific treatment.

FITS
See Convulsions.

FLATULENCE
Gas in the digestive tract caused by a change in food, damaged food or the wrong diet (e.g. too little fibre), and also allergic reactions, malabsorption, and the pancreas producing too few enzymes leading to inadequate digestion.

In small animals it can be alleviated by human medicines such as medicinal charcoal and kaolin. Bismuth nitrate is particularly good.

A standard formula is:

Bismuth carbonate	4 grams
Sodium bi-carbonate	3 grams
Magnesium carbonate	3 grams

Mix and divide into four doses. For a dog weighing 35 lb (15.8 kg.) give one every eight hours.

It is most important to put the diet right and if flatulence continues, consult your vet.

In horses and donkeys some flatulence is normal. As long as gas is being passed simply check on diet and quality of food. If severe it may cause colic (see Colic).

FLEAS
There are about a thousand species, each preferring, but not exclusively, a particular host. For example, cat fleas can bite humans and rabbit fleas will bite dogs. They are more annoying than dangerous. They can cause mild or severe irritation but seldom, if ever, endanger life.

Symptoms are scratching and sometimes scabs, especially along the back. Flea dirt – pinhead-sized black particles – can be found in the coat. For confirmation, place these particles on wet blotting paper and a red bloodstain will develop.

Fleas are wingless insects with flat sides and with strong legs for jumping. They suck the host's blood frequently and rest in the bedding, where they lay large oval eggs. Eggs hatch in from 2 to 12 days into minute caterpillar-like larvae which feed on organic material. In two weeks they have moulted twice and spin a cocoon in which to pupate for another week before they become adult – the whole life cycle taking between three and five weeks.

It is important, therefore, to destroy the bedding where the animal sleeps as well as to spray or dust the animal with one of the newer effective parasiticides at three-week intervals, several times.

Follow the manufacturers' instructions carefully.

FLU

See Influenza.

FOREIGN BODIES

Found mainly in cats and dogs. Fur balls are dealt with separately (see Fur balls).

Cats will play with cotton and may swallow an attached needle which can lodge in the throat or mouth, and occasionally it may pass lower down the digestive tract. A needle or bone in the mouth will make the cat paw at its mouth. If it is in the throat the animal may stretch repeatedly. Less obvious and more serious symptoms of illness are caused if it lodges in the digestive tract.

Dogs play with and swallow stones, conkers and even small balls, and other objects which cause severe symptoms if they become lodged, usually in the stomach or intestines. Small chop bones may lodge at the entrance to the stomach.

In all cases expert help must be sought. Surgical removal is usually necessary.

Horses, unlike cows, rarely swallow without adequate chewing and foreign bodies are rare.

FRACTURES

Broken bones result from injury though there are pathological conditions of bone predisposing spontaneous fracture. There will be unnatural movement and pain. Later, swelling will develop, and in many cases a grating sound when moved. The animal will be disinclined to move, and may not be able to move the affected part. Fractures can be confused with dislocation or sprains.

In most species the limbs are most frequently affected, though in theory any bone can break.

Fracture of the jaw is not uncommon in cats due to jumping down from a high place on to a hard surface. The front legs are unable to take the force of the impact and the jaw hits the hard surface.

It is necessary to take the animal to a vet for diagnosis, which may require an X-ray and treatment. This may be just a matter of realigning the broken bones and setting in plaster. Or it may mean fixing with steel plates or pins. Fractures of limb bones in the horse and donkey can often be treated. In the past it was the custom to put the animal down.

FROG
The soft triangular structure of the underside of the hoof of the horse or donkey. It helps to cushion the impact of foot on to ground. The foot should be kept clean and not continually in wet faeces and urine. Otherwise the frog may become infected and begin to rot.

FROSTBITE
Rarely if ever affects animals in Britain. Extremities such as tail or toes are vulnerable due to poor circulation. It may not be noticed until the skin becomes dry and peels. Treat as for wounds.

FUNGAL INFECTION
Tortoises can get mycotic infection in the eye and the digestive system. They can be treated. Consult your vet. (See Eye and Enteritis).

FUNGUS
One of the commonest diseases affecting fresh-water fish. The symptom is the growth of thin threads of dirty white colour on skin or fins that may resemble cotton wool. It usually follows an injury or damage by a parasite. There are a great many species of moulds and many are present in the water. It spreads slowly on the affected

fish but rapidly on a dead fish.

Treatment: make sure the environment is suitable, i.e. that water temperature, PH, hardness and aeration are normal (see Water). Treat the fungus locally by taking the fish out of water on to a smooth surface like a rubber glove, and touch the fungus with a 1:10 solution of iodine or 1:10 mecurochrome 2% in distilled water. A more mild treatment is potassium dichromate 1% solution. Repeat daily till cured or for 10 days. Another treatment is to put the fish in clean water with 0.1 parts per million of malachite green.

FUR BALLS

Can form in the intestines because swallowed hair matts into such large masses that they cannot be passed by the animal. They occur in cats, guinea pigs, hamsters and, much less frequently, in rabbits, horses, and other species.

Because they prevent the passage of faeces these accumulate and slowly poison the animal. One can be deceived because faecal fluid may seep past the impaction, giving the impression that there is no blockage. The abdomen becomes distended, though the animal is off its food and may be vomiting.

If the animal is not seriously sick, dosing with liquid paraffin or vegetable oil may lubricate the bowel enough to allow the mass to be passed. The dose for an adult cat is a dessertspoonful three times daily. And for smaller animals in proportion to size. There is no danger of overdosing. Massaging the abdomen may help to lengthen the mass and reduce its diameter. Otherwise expert help should be sought, and surgery may be required to remove the fur ball.

Cats, however, regurgitate smaller fur balls from time to time, and this is quite normal.

GANGRENE
See Skin.

GAS
In abdomen (see Flatulence).

Occasionally in the dog the stomach can become displaced and swell up with gas. The belly becomes distended and the animal is in a serious condition due to excessive pressure on the lungs.

Seek veterinary help at once as it is a dangerous condition.

GASTRITIS

Inflammation of the stomach, which may be caused by caustic material or damaged or bad food. It may also be caused by an infection in the stomach, or be due to specific diseases such as distemper or pyometra.

If mild, the animal is simply off its food and appears dull, and may have a rise in body temperature. More severe gastritis causes vomiting of fluid that looks like saliva – clear and bubbly – and may contain streaks of fresh blood once the stomach contents have been expelled. There may or may not be a rise in body temperature. Often gastritis is associated with enteritis which causes other symptoms (see Enteritis). The animal can become dehydrated and develop shock, so seek veterinary help unless the condition is mild.

Mild cases can be treated with Bisodol or another human gastric sedative at a dose rate in relation to weight – a large labrador will require an adult human dose. (See also Vomiting).

Inflammation of the stomach in tortoises can be caused by a mycotic infection and feeding the wrong foods, which decompose in the stomach. The animal is sluggish and off its food and there may possibly be diarrhoea due to an accompanying enteritis. It is best to consult the vet for accurate diagnosis and treatment.

GESTATION

(See Breeding for tortoises).

GILLS

The lungs of the fish. Water is pulled through and oxygen extracted: at the same time carbon dioxide is given off, as in respiration in mammals. They are normally a reddish colour. To prevent gills becoming clogged with particles of food and debris there are gill rakes to provide a fine mesh sieve.

Damage to gills causes respiratory problems that can lead to death. Injury can be followed by a fungus infection (gill rot) which will spread and cause suffocation. It is rare in aquarium fish.

A parasite called a fluke can affect the gills and cause serious respiratory problems. Several treatments have been used: 1) Salt – in a solution of 15g. (½ oz.) in each litre (1.7 pints) of water and putting the fish in the solution for 20 minutes.
2) Formalin – solution of 1–2 ml. of 40% solution in 10 litres (17.5 pints) of water and immersing the fish in it for 10–20 minutes.
3) Ammonia – a 1 in 2,000 solution and immersing the fish for 20 minutes, followed by immersion in a solution of methylene blue (1 ml. of the 1% solution in 9 litres (15.8 pints) of water) for a further 10 minutes or so. The 1% solution of methylene blue can be bought; for the ammonia solution you should reckon 1 ml. of strong ammonia purchased from the chemist to 5 gals (22.7 litres) of water.

Pale gills are a sign of disease.

GROOMING

Many animals groom themselves or each other. Single animals and especially those with long and thick coats will benefit from grooming, which will remove loose hair and stimulate blood circulation in the skin, and give the coat a glossy, healthy-looking appearance. Always finish by brushing with the lie of the coat. Combing is also useful.

The coats of horses and donkeys often become ingrained with hay seeds, awns and dust, especially when housed in the winter. And horses, unlike cats and dogs, sweat all over. So grooming is especially useful and should be a daily practice taking half an hour once the animal has cooled down. Begin at the head and work backwards and downwards, using a brush and comb. It may be necessary to scrape mud from the coat before brushing. The curry comb is used to clean the bristles of the brush. Always clean and disinfect the brush and comb regularly, and so far as is possible, don't use on strange animals or use other brushes and combs on your animals, as this can spread skin infections such as ringworm (see Ringworm).

GUMS

Inflammation is called gingivitis; it is caused by various infections and poisons, and follows some diseases such as distemper, leptospirosis and diabetes. Symptoms are reddening of the gums and possibly bleeding; they may be ulcerated and painful, causing difficulty in feeding. There may be excessive salivation, and the breath will have a bad smell. Formation of tartar in older animals can cause accumulation of food at the junction with the gums, resulting in inflammation and bad breath. Tartar can be removed and often there are sound teeth underneath. Inflammation may then resolve, and if not a course of antibiotic will help.

The molar teeth of horses and donkeys continue to grow and sometimes the outer edges of the upper teeth and the inner edges of the lower teeth become worn to a sharp edge which damages the inner cheek surfaces. The sharp edges can be rasped down by the vet (see Teeth).

Damaged teeth or spaces between teeth can result in food materials become impacted and causing inflammation.

The incisor teeth of rodents continue to grow and wear down with use. If one tooth is damaged, the opposing tooth is not worn down and may grow so long it prevents the animal closing its mouth to chew.

Diet is most important in keeping gums and teeth healthy. It must contain the correct nutrients in proper balance (see Diet). And it should provide enough of the right material to chew upon: good hay for horses, donkeys and other herbivores, and raw bones of the right size for carnivores to chew, especially when young and growing.

HABITS

Are acquired and can be lost or altered. Instinctive behaviour is inherited but can be adapted or displaced. Some behavioural problems are a mixture of both.

Habits result from training which may be imposed by the environment or by the owner.

A dog may form the habit of chasing after motor cyclists, and a cat of using a litter box. The owner can break the former and reinforce the latter, and form new habits such as keeping to the side of the road, by careful training. In fact because it is natural to form habits it is important to think carefully about how you react with your pet. You may unwittingly cause it to acquire habits you don't like – for example, biting strangers or using the furniture as a scratching post.

Even small species will respond to attention. Goldfish soon get to know when it is feeding time.

Habits usually take at least six weeks to form and will take six weeks to break or change, with constant reinforcement.

Training should begin as soon after weaning as possible and be continued frequently, throughout the day if possible. Attention time and memory time are short.

HAEMATOMA
See Blood blister.

HAEMORRHAGE
Bleeding caused by injury or the rupture of blood vessels due to tumours or ulceration.

Generalised haemorrhage in many parts of the body is caused by some poisons such as Warfarin, by allergic shock, by some diseases like hepatitis, and by haemophilia to some extent.

Bleeding from an artery spurts in time with the heartbeat. Bleeding from veins flows and the blood is darker, and bleeding from capillary vessels oozes. Cut vessels bleed more freely than torn vessels.

A little blood when spread about looks like a massive haemorrhage. Don't panic. But if the blood is spurting or flowing freely from a fresh cut it can be stopped immediately by firm pressure in almost all cases. Digital pressure is the best method, as cloth soaks up blood and pressure is not so easily applied to the bleeding point. A vet can then be called or a pressure pad applied. This is simply a piece of clean cloth folded or containing a wad of cotton wool to make it an egg-shaped pad, which is placed on the bleeding point and bandaged tightly in place. As the bandage may interfere with circulation professional help should be sought at once, and if not available, the bandage loosened but the pad held tight, to allow circulation to flow for a few minutes without allowing the vessel to bleed.

So long as the blood clots all other external bleeding can be stopped by firm (not tight) bandaging (see Bandaging and also Wounds).

Cases of generalised haemorrhage should be taken to the vet for diagnosis and treatment.

HAIR BALLS
See Fur Balls.

HALITOSIS
See Breath.

HEALTH
Signs in mammals are: good appetite, plenty of energy, a bright alert eye, shiny unmatted hair, fresh-smelling breath, and normal faeces and urine. In birds, the feathers should be well preened.

However, when animals and birds moult in the autumn or spring the hair may come out in tufts and feathers be lost, which may give the pet an unkempt appearance.

Signs of a healthy tortoise are as follows. When resting, the head and limbs are not completely withdrawn but in line with the shell border, they may even be protruding out of the shell at rest. It is active and feeding well and feels heavy when lifted. When moving, the shell is carried horizontally. Movements are strong not jerky, and the animal stops occasionally to smell the ground. If in doubt, try the float test by slowly lowering it into deep water and it should remain level. If it tilts there is an internal problem, and if it sinks it may be eggbound or have swallowed gravel.

Provided environmental temperature is within the normal range the reflex reactions of the tortoise should be rapid when it is touched and it should make active attempts to right itself when turned over. A normal healthy tortoise can support its weight suspended on its front legs when they are hooked over one's fingers. A weak tortoise cannot do this. And an unhealthy tortoise rests with front limbs well withdrawn into the shell, or alternatively the front legs are splayed out and the head withdrawn well inside its shell.

HEART

The body's blood circulation pump is subject to various disease problems. In the majority of cases animals take enough exercise if it is possible to do so. But they are at the mercy of the diet provided by their owners.

Because they don't smoke or drink they escape some heart disease problems. They can suffer from inflammation of the heart muscle, the valves, the lining of the heart, and the sac in which the heart lies. And congenital defects and disorders of the nerve conduction can also affect animals.

Heart failure may be acute and sudden. The animal collapses unconscious and no heartbeat can be felt. Place the animal on its side and firmly press the thorax over the heart sufficiently to squeeze it and immediately relax, and after one or two seconds repeat. This cardiac massage may restart the heart.

Chronic heart failure is due to reduced efficiency caused by a number of conditions. Symptoms are breathlessness, possibly a cough especially at night, a weak pulse, and possibly an enlarged liver and fluid in the abdomen. The gums may be pale and there is loss of weight. It is necessary to consult a vet for accurate diagnosis upon which proper treatment is based. Obesity can put an extra burden on the heart. Stress is also harmful. A reduction of salt in the diet is recommended.

Inflammation of the heart is caused by an infection, usually by bacteria. There will probably be an increase in body temperature, increased heart rates, tiredness and pale mucous membranes. Consult the vet at once. Antibiotic therapy works well. Rest is essential.

Heart disease is particularly serious in horses and donkeys for they may collapse suddenly while being ridden and throw the rider.

HEAT

Or Oestrus periods in female animals occur at regular intervals, coinciding with development of the egg or ovum. There is a slight rise in body temperature at the height of the period, which lasts for different lengths of time in each species.

Amongst pets it is longest in the bitch, lasting up to three weeks.

In the horse it lasts only 1–3 days. Signs vary according to the species.

The mare may show a slight change in temperature, becoming more skittish, and close to the time when she will permit mating she may urinate frequently, small amounts of urine.

The bitch begins to lose small amounts of watery-looking blood from the vagina about 10 days before the eggs are shed. The bleeding stops for 3–4 days and is replaced by clear mucous and then bleeding begins again for another week. The bitch emits an odour which is attractive to dogs, which can pick it up from fairly far away. Heat normally occurs twice per year, in spring and autumn.

The queen vocalises when she is on heat and males are attracted. It lasts three weeks and is in three phases. In the first five days she becomes more affectionate. The second phase lasts 7–10 days, when she is receptive and can conceive. She presents her rear end and treads with her back legs. The third phase lasts 3–5 days and she is less and less receptive. Unlike the bitch she may have two or more cycles like this one after another in the spring and again in the autumn. If however she conceives, cycles will cease.

Rabbits have no cycle but can remain on heat for long periods. The vulva appears slightly enlarged and purplish when receptive, and does dip their back when ready for mating. Ovulation follows and is induced by mating.

Guinea pigs' oestrus cycle is of 15 days' duration, and just over half way through the female becomes receptive and ovulation takes place.

Small rodents also have heat periods that are short. The hamster comes on heat every four days.

See also Pregnancy.

HEAT STROKE

Rarely affects free animals. It occurs in dogs when confined in a hot environment with no ventilation, for example, in a car. Not often seen in cats or other small animals. Occurs in horses in hot humid climates when crowded in yards or trucks in the sun. Can also occur when they are worked hard in hot sunshine, especially if short of drinking water. The animal becomes distressed with rapid breathing and a considerable rise in body temperature. The pulse is fast and weak and sweating may have reduced (see Sweating), or even stopped. The pupils become dilated and the animal staggers and may fall down and struggle. Later muscle spasms may develop and death can occur soon afterwards. There may be diarrhoea.

Treatment must be prompt. Small animals can be immersed (except for head) in cold water. Cold water can be sprayed, hosed, or bucketed on to horses. If symptoms are severe call the vet in case heart stimulants are required. The animal should respond fairly quickly.

Antibiotics may be given to prevent infection developing.

If a tortoise has collapsed or appears very weak, and both it and the environment are very warm, suspect heat stroke. Tortoises can only regulate their temperature by seeking shade and cooler areas. Heat stroke is often fatal. Treat by gently bathing in cool water and then placing in an environment of 70°F (21°C). Less severe cases may be placed in a cooler environment and sprayed every hour or so with cold water from an atomiser.

HEEL

Applies only to horses and donkeys. It is that part of the back of the foot just above the sole to the rear of the hoof.

Cracked heel is inflamed horizontal cracks with thickened edges of the skin in the hollow of the heel. It is due to allowing the area to be continually wet, and the resulting chapping becomes infected. The animal is lame. Treatment is to wash the area with good-quality soap to remove crust and then dry thoroughly and apply zinc oxide ointment and repeat daily.

Greasy heel is seborrhoea – an excess secretion of the oil glands of the skin accompanied by inflammation of the skin. It is a form of chronic dermatitis (see Skin and Dermatitis). The cause is not known but it mainly occurs in heavy horses with thick long hair in the heels, which are not cleaned and groomed properly. The area may have a bad odour due to bacterial infection. For treatment, clip the hair close to the skin, wash with good soap thoroughly and apply zinc oxide ointment. If it doesn't respond, consult your vet.

HEPATITIS

Inflammation of the liver. May be acute with symptoms of vomiting, loss of appetite, dehydration and pain in the liver, which lies in the upper abdomen and partially behind the ribs. It may be chronic, with vague symptoms of malaise, lethargy, poor appetite, and possibly enlargement of the liver and jaundice.

There are specific liver infections such as canine hepatitis and leptospirosis for which there are preventative vaccines (see Vaccination). But forms of poisoning, cancer, injury and diabetes mellitus can also cause the disease. It is necessary to consult your vet for accurate diagnosis and proper treatment.

HERNIA

The protrusion of abdominal contents through a hole in the wall of the belly.

Umbilical hernia occurs where the umbilical cord was attached, and scrotal hernia is at the opening through which pass the cord and blood vessels of the testicle, and abdominal contents enter the scrotum.

Artificial hernias can occur when the abdominal wall or the diaphragm is broken in an accident. If the hole is large the bowels escape and lie beneath the skin, or in diaphragmatic hernia the bowels enter the chest and interfere with breathing.

There is an inherited tendency to suffer from umbilical and scrotal hernias, which can vary in size, and the contents can be massaged back into the abdomen. As there is always a danger, when bowels escape and lie under the skin, of their swelling and closing off the passage of food material, it is wise to consult your vet, who may advise an operation. Artificial hernia should always be seen by your vet.

HIBERNATION

Many tortoises die during or immediately after hibernation. The three species normally kept as pets in Britain come from around the Mediterranean basin where the climate is warmer. In the wild these species may hibernate for short periods only, so if they can be kept warm enough, there is no need for them to hibernate. Otherwise

there are several important points:
1) Don't allow a tortoise less than 4 inches (10 cm.) long to hibernate.
2) The tortoise should be in good bodily condition, with plenty of fat reserves, to survive.
3) The stomach should be empty, otherwise food in the digestive tract will decompose and poison the animal.
4) The length of hibernation should not be too long.
5) When it begins to awaken, put it in a warm environment at once and check that the mouth is not stuck shut.
6) Put on normal diet.

Preparation for hiberation is important. Feed well until animal is fat. This can be calculated by measuring the length, weight and height in inches – adding these figures together and multiplying by 4.8 ounces, to give the optimum weight. If the weight is less than this figure, do not allow to hibernate.

If it is fat enough, feed only citrus fruit for four weeks to clear out the digestive system, in an environmental temperature of 70°F (21°C). Then reduce the temperature to 65°F (18°C) and finally 60°F (15°C) and the tortoise will become lethargic. After two days place in a box with a thick layer of sphagnum moss and dry leaves, or straw, into which it can burrow. Move box to a dry draught-proof room or shed with a temperature of no more than 45°F (7°C).

Check every 24 hours for running eyes, blocked nose, etc., during the first week, then every two days, then weekly for a month, and then monthly. Don't disturb the animal.

As the temperature rises the tortoise will become more active. Place in a temperature of 60°F (15°C) and gradually increase up to 78°F (26°C) when proper feeding commences.

HICCUPS

Rhythmic spasms of the diaphragm due to irritation of the nerve supply. The cause is not known. It may be associated with heavy infestation of worms, or gulping food down too quickly by young animals. It is not common in animals. It will usually stop in a short time.

If prolonged, dose with a stomach sedative (see treatment for Gastritis).

HOUSING

All animals kept as pets require housing to protect them from bad weather.

Dry coats are a fairly good insulation against cold, but when wet, insulation is very much reduced. So they are susceptible to wet, cold weather, especially when resting or sleeping.

Horses and donkeys require a dry bed though the housing can be open provided it shelters the animal from rain and the prevailing cold winds. Animals which are normally housed do not grow a thick winter coat, and they, and animals which have been clipped, need more protection like a stable and perhaps a rug in particularly cold weather, and also when taken out in bad weather.

Dogs may be quite comfortable in an outside kennel provided it is draught-proof and the entrance is facing south, or it is sheltered and is lined with straw to make a snug bed.

Dogs and cats kept indoors should have beds slightly raised above the floor to avoid draughts.

Gerbils, hamsters and guinea pigs can stand a dry cold but are susceptible to wet cold. They should be housed in dry accommodation – a cage in the house or a dry shed.

Rabbits are also susceptible to wet cold, but they seem less susceptible to draughts. They are often housed in hutches in the garden. They must have dry sleeping quarters. They will use a wire run during the day but keep moving it to prevent the ground becoming a mud bath.

Straw is the best bedding material as it is a good insulation material, fairly free of dust, and less liked by fleas and lice. It can be burnt and replaced periodically. It is not dangerous if eaten by herbivorous animals.

Dry peat is good for horses and donkeys and can be used for other animals. But it can get dusty.

Shredded paper is also good and easier to obtain in towns. Remove and replace whenever wet or dirty, and at least every few weeks.

Synthetic fibres are not good, for the animal may chew and eat some with harmful effects.

Wood shavings and sawdust are not good as they may contain

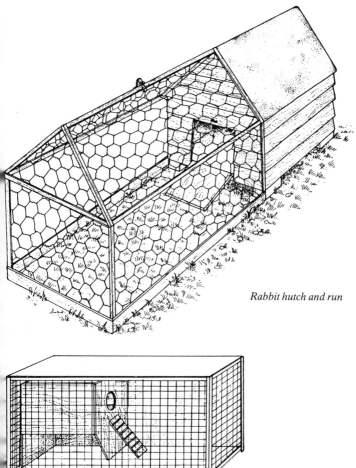

Rabbit hutch and run

Hamster cage

creosote or other harmful chemicals.

Tortoises are sensitive animals and need a quiet, secluded box for resting (see Accommodation). Unless the box outside is heated the tortoise must be brought into a warmer environment when the outside temperature falls below 65° (18°C).

For fish, see Tank and Water.

INCONTINENCE

Frequent involuntary passing of urine can occur in young dogs due to nervousness. Occasionally it is a congenital defect – the animal is born with an abnormal urethra or bladder that cannot retain urine normally.

When it occurs in animals that have until then been normal the cause can be a stone in the bladder or urethra, an infection of those parts, a tumour, or a result of surgery to that area, or a hormone imbalance after speying.

It should be distinguished from voluntary, frequent passing of urine, which in the male dog or cat is a method of marking their territory, and can develop into a psychological problem when a well-cared-for pet is suddenly ignored, as, for example, when a baby arrives in the house, or the owner is taken ill, or goes out to work instead of being at home.

Treatment depends on the cause and your vet should be consulted.

INCUBATION

(See Breeding for tortoises).

INDIGESTION

A mild upset of the digestive process usually caused by eating damaged food, garbage, or indigestible material. Overeating is another cause, especially in horses and donkeys. It can accompany mild febrile infection.

Treatment for horses and donkeys is either a warm bran mash or a dose of kaolin and sodium bicarbonate. Food (not water) should be withheld till it has gone.

Dogs and cats can be given a stomach sedative as recommended for gastritis (see Gastritis).

Small animals respond to medicinal liquid paraffin and withholding food for a day or two.

INFLAMMATION

The body's reaction to injury and infection. Blood supply to the inflamed part or organ is increased and white cells – the body's defenders – multiply and migrate to the part, which becomes swollen, red, hot and painful.

Treatment depends on the cause. Cold compresses will help control inflammation from bruising and burns if applied at once.

Infections and allergies are best treated by your vet. (See also under each organ, e.g. Eye, Liver, Stomach, etc.)

INFLUENZA

An infection caused by a virus. There are many types. Some are almost specific to one species of animal whilst others can infect more than one species. The virus causing flu in horses and donkeys is similar to that which affects humans. The animal goes off its food, appears depressed, has an elevated body temperature, and has a cough and nasal discharge. Other organs are affected and the animal is seriously ill and can take weeks to recover.

Treatment consists of rest and good nursing, for the heart can be affected, and if the animal is exercised too soon permanent damage can occur. Antibiotics are useful if secondary bacterial infection occurs.

There is a good vaccine available to prevent flu, so consult your vet.

Dogs can get a flu-like disease which is one cause of kennel cough. Flu symptoms are the same as in the horse and donkey and a vaccine is available.

Cats get flu which, in addition to the usual symptoms, can cause sneezing and head shaking, and sometimes bleeding from the nose. A vaccine is available.

Not enough is known about small species but it is highly likely that they get flu of a type that may be specific to them, and the secondary infection follows causing nasal discharge and respiratory symptoms. Consult your vet. Vaccines are not available.

Birds can get respiratory disease but not the flu virus. Psittacosis causes respiratory symptoms. (See Nose, Trachea and Lungs).

INJECTION

A method of administering a medicine. It can be given directly into the blood stream (intravenously), or into the muscle (intramuscular), or under the skin (subcutaneously). Sites are chosen to avoid damage to nerves and blood vessels.

The horse and donkey can be injected intravenously in the jugular vein in the neck; intramuscularly in the muscle of the rump (danger of being kicked) or in the muscle in front of the chest above the brisket, or in the neck muscle; and subcutaneously under the skin of the neck, or by the shoulder.

Dogs and cats are injected intravenously in the vein on the fore limb; intramuscularly in the muscle of the hind limb from the rear; and subcutaneously in the scruff of the neck.

Small species are injected in the vein of the fore limb and in the rabbit a good vein can be found in its large ear. Intramuscular and subcutaneous sites are the same as for cats and dogs.

The syringe and needle must be sterile and the skin of the animal is usually swabbed with methylated spirit or other skin antiseptic.

INJURY

See Wounds, Burns, Fractures, Bruising, Caustic Damage.

Though tortoises seem well protected they suffer injuries not infrequently. Injuries to the limbs and neck can be caused by the animal's attempts to climb wire netting, or being bitten by a dog or another tortoise. Damage to the shell can be caused by a dog bite or being dropped. Legs can be fractured by getting wedged in a box or fence, or travelling crate. A broken leg is often dragged and the animal is lame. Expert help should be sought.

A transverse line across the shell is not necessarily a fracture. In some species of tortoise parts of the shell are not joined together by bone, but not in the species usually kept as pets.

Paraphimosis – extrusion and swelling of the penis – is not uncommon in young tortoises. The cause is excitement causing protrusion of the penis which is then injured by a bite from another tortoise. Swelling prevents it from going back. You must consult your vet for treatment.

The bodies of fish are covered with a fine transparent sensitive membrane. It covers the scales and the eye and is particularly liable to injury, which often allows infections to get a hold. The dry skin of a human hand will damage this membrane. It is advisable to wear a rubber glove or smooth plastic glove when handling fish.

KERATITIS
See Eye.

KIDNEY
The kidneys purify the body fluids and help keep the correct balance of minerals and water.

One kidney is sufficient but nature provides two because when kidney cells are damaged they are not replaced. Injury can occur from run-over accidents in small animals but the kidneys are well protected, lying close under the spine.

Inflammation of the kidneys is called nephritis. It can be acute or chronic and is caused by infections, toxaemia or poisons.

Acute – symptoms are depression, off food, increased thirst but passing little urine, pain along back, occasional vomiting and a rise in body temperature. There may be diarrhoea or constipation, and when very serious convulsions occur it is not long before death.

Chronic – symptoms are depression but probably a normal body temperature, appetite normal or reduced, drinking a lot, and passing a lot of urine. There may be vomiting and probably dehydration. Later anaemia may develop and the coat becomes rough.

Treatment depends on the cause and veterinary help should be sought as soon as possible. A specially prepared diet for dogs and cats with nephritis is available.

LAMENESS
A symptom of pain in a limb, or it can be mechanical and painless.

Pain makes the animal rest the limb and so prevent further injury and allow healing. Rest is a major factor in the healing process.

The animal may have a slight limp (taking less weight on the affected leg), or it may be so severe that the limb does not take any weight. Causes are arthritis, dislocation, fracture, inflammation of tendons, synovical membranes, muscles, ligaments or nerves, rupture of tendons, rickets, hip dysplasia, nerve paralysis and ankylosis or fixation of a joint. Other causes are injuries to the foot – wounds, thorn punctures, interdigital cysts, laminitis and also inguinal hernia, and specific disease conditions of the bones and soft tissues of the limb such as cancer (see Arthritis).

Treatment depends on accurate diagnosis. Unless the cause is obvious and simple consult your vet.

If painkillers are given it is important to rest the animal or more damage may result.

LAMINITIS

Inflammation of the sensitive tissue behind the hoof, therefore not found in small animal pets.

It is caused by overeating of either fresh rich grass or concentrates. It can also follow retained afterbirth when foaling, and drinking a lot of cold water immediately after exercise.

Any or all of the feet may be affected: they are hot and very painful and the horse tries to rest the limbs.

Chronic laminitis can follow the acute stage and the animal is not so lame nor is the hoof hot, but because the blood supply to the hoof is affected, changes occur in the shape of the hoof. It tends to grow out concavely and, if not trimmed, the toes turn up and the sole of the hoof drops.

Treatment of acute laminitis should be prompt. The vet can inject but the animal should be kept indoors on a soft bed, food reduced to hay, and the shoes removed. Chronic laminitis may respond to trimming of the hoof by a good farrier, and sometimes special shoes are used.

LARYNGEAL PARALYSIS

Due to damage to the nerve supplying the larynx. This may be caused by infection, injury or cancer, and it may be congenital.

Symptoms are a change in vocal sounds, and, if severe, some difficulty in breathing.

In equines the condition called roaring is due to paralysis of the left side of the larynx in 80% of cases. The cause is not known. The symptoms are difficulty in breathing and making a characteristic noise, hence the name. This causes poor ventilation, lack of oxygen and early tiring.

The only treatment is an operation.

LARYNGITIS

Can be caused by injury from a foreign body, infection and cancer. The animal loses its appetite and may be breathless, and have alteration in vocal sounds. There may be a cough and the infectious type can cause a rise in body temperature.

It is necessary to consult your vet for accurate diagnosis and treatment.

All species get laryngitis but it is not common.

LAXATIVES

Substances used to relieve bowel stasis and constipation. There are three types:
  1) Substances that increase the volume or bulk of intestinal contents.
  2) Substances that lubricate.
  3) Substances that stimulate or irritate the intestines.

1. To herbivorous animals on a dry food diet fresh green vegetation is laxative.

A bran mash is suitable for horses and donkeys. (Take a double handful of bran in a bucket, pour on a kettle of boiling water and stir into a porridge, add a small cup of molasses and water to make a warm fluid, and give warm to drink.

Epsom salts – 200gm. for a large horse in a pint or two of water. For small animals, 4gm. for every 5kg. (11 lbs) body weight, diluted in water the strength must not be less than 5% (1 part in 20 of water). It can be more concentrated (say 1 part in 10) for dogs and cats, for it will add bulk to the intestines.

2. The best lubricant is medicinal liquid paraffin though vegetable oils can also be used but they may be digested and absorbed. The dose for a large riding horse is 1 litre and for a donkey ½ litre (1 pint).

Large dogs should get 2 dessertspoons three times daily. Small dogs ½–1 dessertspoon three times daily, and cats 2 teaspoons. Smaller animals can be given ½ teaspoon or less according to size. Liquid paraffin is harmless and even three or four times the normal dose will do no harm.

3. Castor oil is the main medicine in this group. There are other compounds but because they act by irritating the bowels they should not be used unless prescribed by a vet.

LEPTOSPIROSIS

A bacterial disease that can affect several species.

In the horse there is an uncommon eye disease associated with leptospira.

Leptospirosis is common in dogs. There are two types, one affecting the kidneys and the other the liver. Symptoms are of illness, fever, thirst, abdominal pain and vomiting. The animal is depressed and may later become jaundiced. There may be ulceration of the mouth and uraemia (see Uraemia).

It responds well to antibiotics, particularly penicillin and streptomycin if caught early. If not, or if the infection is very strong, there may be permanent damage to the kidneys leading to chronic nephritis.

You must consult your vet as soon as possible. A vaccine is available (see Vaccines).

LETHARGY

See Tiredness.

LEUKAEMIA

An abnormal increase in the numbers of white blood cells. One form may be a type of cancer. It is rare in horses and donkeys and not common in other species.

Symptoms resemble anaemia – lethargy, weakness and loss of appetite.

Cats get an infectious leukaemia caused by a virus and it is not uncommon. Symptoms are fever, loss of appetite, weakness, anaemia and wasting. There may be enlargement of the liver and spleen with vomiting and possibly diarrhoea. It can affect the kidneys and cause acute renal failure (see Nephritis). Another form can cause coughing and it can affect the eyes.

Various treatments have been tried, and some, for example corticosteroids, can bring about remission for a time.

LICE

Flattened wingless insects entirely parasitic. There are two main groups: sucking lice which suck blood, and biting lice which eat material on the surface of the skin. The eggs are glued to the hair of the host. They hatch into immature lice which also feed on blood and become mature in 1–2 weeks and in turn begin breeding. They irritate the host which may lose condition. Infection occurs with close contact of host animals.

Horses and donkeys get three species but one is uncommon.

Dogs get infested with two species and cats with one, which is a biting louse.

Birds can get a number of species and all are biting lice.

Treatment nowadays is effective with new preparations but follow the instructions carefully and exactly, as overdosing is harmful. Change the bedding frequently and burn it in case it contains some lice though they usually spend all their lives on the host.

Aquarium fish can be parasitised with lice which are introduced on other fish or plants. They look like small plaice and are attached to the host, mainly around the gills and throat region, with suckers. They feed on body fluids, wounding the fish and causing loss of condition. They can swim freely and move from one host to another. They can be picked off, but if there are many it is easier to place the fish in a solution of 1 teaspoon of Dettol to 2 gallons (9 litres) of water (at the same temperature as the water in their tank), and the lice will drop off at once. Do not leave the fish in this solution longer than is necessary and no longer than two minutes. Watch carefully for signs of distress.

Fish can also become infested with a crustacean called a fish louse (Argulus). It is free-swimming and looks like the lice that affects mammals. The best treatment is an organic phosphorous compound, and don't forget that because they are free-living, the tank must be treated too, with a strength of 0.025 part per million of Mastoten, or its equivalent.

A 'shotgun' approach used in America is a cocktail of:

Formalin	25 parts per million
Organophosphate	0.25 parts per million
Metronidazole	5 parts per million

all of which can be obtained from a veterinary surgeon. The method of use is to place the fish in this solution for a day and then change the water and repeat two or three more times.

LIGAMENTS
Hold bones together at many joints. They are strong bands of tissue and are not elastic like tendons.

A sprain is a damaged ligament, resulting from injury. The ligament may be torn from its attachment, or partly pulled apart. There is acute pain, swelling and heat in the area.

Firm bandaging (take care not to cut off the blood supply) and rest are the best treatment. If it is very severe consult the vet.

LIGHT
Necessary for the growth of the plants in the fish tank and the light should be placed close to the water for 8–10 hours daily. A 60–100 watt light is sufficient for the average tank.

LIGHTNING STRIKE
Animals are much more easily killed by lightning than human beings. It simply stops the heart. And unless the heart is quickly started again the animal will die. If you see the accident occur, treat as for electric shock and heart failure.

LIVER
A complex organ that is the body's main factory for processing nutrients and detoxifying poisonous substances. It can be damaged

by toxins, and become inflamed by infection – see Hepatitis.

Damage to the liver can produce many symptoms, particularly loss of appetite and depression.

LUNGS

A light, spongy, elastic organ where the blood takes up oxygen and gives off carbon dioxide. The lining of the thousands of little cavities is a sensitive mucous membrane which is susceptible to injury from irritants and from infection, causing inflammation (see Pneumonia).

MAMMARY GLAND

Subject to infection (called mastitis), tumours, cancer and injury.

Mammary glands only complete their development in the latter part of pregnancy, and after weaning they become much smaller, especially in domestic pets. They may also increase in size and become hard and painful in false pregnancy, which occurs about nine weeks after heat in bitches but is rare in other species.

Mares and jennys occasionally get mastitis when in milk. It is dangerous for both mother and foal. The mother is especially vulnerable if the foal is born dead. It causes a fever, depression, lack of appetite, loss of milk production, and the gland is hot, swollen and painful.

Dogs and cats seem more susceptible though it is not common. Symptoms are the same.

Mastitis can occur in smaller species but is rare.

Treatment required is antibiotic by injection, so a vet must be consulted. Bathing with hot but bearable water may give some relief.

The infection can be chronic and the only symptom is a hard swelling. Antibiotic treatment is then not quite so effective because it cannot so easily reach the bacterial cause.

Cancer and the slower-growing tumour are not uncommon in older bitches but are rare in other species. Surgical treatment may be necessary.

False pregnancy can be treated with hormones by injection or by mouth, so consult your vet.

Injury can cause bruising with perhaps internal bleeding. The area is painful, hot and swollen. In the early stages cold compresses of crushed ice in a cloth may reduce swelling. Later, bathing with warm water will ease the pain. Watch carefully in case it becomes infected – it will suddenly become more swollen and painful and the animal may have a fever.

MANGE

A disease of the skin caused by a group of very small insects which either burrow into the skin or live on the surface, and a few species live inside the respiratory system of birds. Some species are host specific, most are not.

Horses and donkeys can become infected with several main types of mange.

Demodectic mange is not common. It is found in the lower half of the neck and very occasionally in the glands of the eye. It causes scaly and pustular skin.

The form that burrows into the skin (sarcoptes) can occasionally also affect humans, and is found anywhere on the body. It is the most serious form affecting horses and donkeys. The mites seek body fluid and cause marked irritation which leads to scratching and biting at the area, and loss of hair. Later the reaction worsens because local sensitivity develops. Even small areas of mange may cause deterioration in health, and if large areas are affected the animal will lose weight.

The form that lives on the surface of the skin eats dead cells and skin secretions. The skin of the host is not so badly affected and doesn't become thickened. The areas affected are the top of the neck, the saddle region, and the base of the tail. Another form affects the feet in the fetlock region and rarely higher up. Horny scales appear and the horse stamps its feet and bites the area.

Dogs are susceptible to all three types. The burrowing type most frequently occurs on the head but spreads rapidly to the rest of the body and seriously affects the animal's health. Demodectic mange which also burrows, but into the skin glands, is serious for it can spread all over the body. It causes a scaly, intensely itchy skin that becomes wrinkled as the hair falls out. Later pustules can form, usually on the abdomen or inside the legs, and become infected with bacteria. The dog develops a repulsive smell which resembles that of mice.

Another species of mite – the ear mite – lives in the external ear canal and causes intense irritation, over-production of wax, and inflammation, and later on bacteria may cause suppuration.

The cat is susceptible to the burrowing type of mange and to demodex, but they are rare. There is another species which attacks only cats and rabbits, affecting the face and ear lobes. The ear canal mite is very common in cats and causes much distress.

Rabbits can get all types of mange and it is possible that other small mammals are susceptible too.

Mites spend all their lives on the host and are passed from one host to another by contact. The female mite lays eggs which hatch in three days into larvae: after six days these moult and become nymphs which in turn moult again to become adults.

Birds are susceptible to a mite that burrows into the shaft of the feathers which then break off. It is called depluming itch. Another type burrows under the scales of the legs, causing inflammation – called scaly leg.

If diagnosed early, treatment is successful in nearly all cases. Modern treatments are very effective but unless used exactly as the manufacturer prescribes they can poison the animal. Badly affected animals can be a problem and demodex is difficult to cure, probably because the mite is buried deep in the skin.

MATING

Can be a problem with pets which are not leading a normal life in that they are not roaming in herds or packs, and some pets kept alone since they were weaned probably feel more at home with humans than with their own species.

Mating occurs when the female comes on heat and at no other time (see Heat). Even when the female is on heat and receptive, care must be exercised.

Mares and jennys will sometimes bite and kick the stallion or jack and can cause serious injury. It is best to introduce the male and female to each other on either side of a strong gate, and only when they are friendly allow them to mate. It is wise to have expert help and whoever leads the animals must be strong enough to pull the animals apart if they begin to kick and bite.

Bitches may turn and bite the dog if not given time to settle. They have been known to bite the dog's penis, causing serious and sometimes irreparable damage.

The tom cat will grasp the scruff of the neck of the female when mating and usually cause no injury. But it is as well to examine the area afterwards and treat if necesary (see Wounds).

Guinea pigs and hamsters can be vicious and a long period of introduction before mating is required.

Gerbils, rats and rabbits are not usually a problem but keep an eye on the developments just in case.

Problems rarely arise when males and females are normally kept together in a group.

Mismating and misalliance can be dealt with by your vet, and in most cases unwanted pregnancy can be successfully terminated. Consult your vet as soon as possible after the event (see Contraception).

For tortoises, see Breeding.

MEDICINES
For methods of administering medicines, see Dosing and Injections.

METRITIS
Inflammation of the uterus, and is rare in virgin animals. It is caused by infection, usually after having given birth. Mild cases only cause a purulent discharge. More severe cases may be accompanied by a fever with depression and loss of milk production.

See also Pyometra.

MILK FEVER
Eclampsia is a type of fit (see Fits) that occurs in the mother soon after she has given birth and is due to a reduction in circulating blood calcium. It is thought that feeding extra calcium and vitamin D in the last third of pregnancy may help to prevent it.

MITES

Other than those causing mange, there is a group of free-living red or orange-coloured minute spider-like creatures. Their larvae suck blood and cause intense irritation. They are particularly a problem in birds. The adults live in cracks and crevices in the cage or housing.

Treatment: wash and disinfect the cage or house thoroughly at intervals of three weeks and the birds may be treated with an insecticide to kill the mites on them.

Small beetle-like grey/black mites are found on the skin, mainly around the head region, of the tortoise. The animal may be restless, rub its head and legs against the shell, and sometimes refuse to feed.

Treat by giving the tortoise a warm bath, allow it to dry, and apply a thin coating of liquid paraffin to the shell as well as the skin, but only to a quarter of the animal at any one time. This will asphyxiate the mites. They are rarely found on tortoises.

MOTION SICKNESS

Can affect dogs and, less commonly, cats, and rarely if ever affects other pets in normal circumstances. Horses and donkeys have been known to be seasick. The animal is restless, begins to salivate, and later may vomit.

Animals are less susceptible if accustomed to travel when young, and if they are allowed to see out. A susceptible dog may travel without being affected if it is allowed to put its head out of the window. Be careful its eyes are not damaged.

Medicinal products to prevent motion sickness are available. Human products like Dramamine have been used in a dose related to body weight.

MOUTH

Susceptible to injury, ulceration (teeth dealt with separately) and infection (called glossitis).

Injury may be caused by biting, sharp objects or splintering woods, burns, stings, or fracture of the jaw by accidents.

Infection may follow injury; burns from chemicals and electricity; dental tartar accumulation; and several generalised diseases such as leptospirosis. Local infection with a virus or fungus or bacteria can occur without obvious injury occurring first. Ulceration can be caused by burns or follow infection, or be associated with chronic nephritis.

Dogs and cats occasionally get a rubber band round the tongue, which swells and becomes infected: if not found soon enough, this may result in gangrene.

Symptoms of injury are salivation, swelling and pain obvious when eating. Infection may cause total loss of appetite and bad breath, as will ulceration.

Treatment depends on the cause. Consult your vet.

A partly open mouth in a tortoise, causing difficulty in feeding, may be due to an overgrown beak. It can be caused by incorrect diet – food too soft, or containing too much or too little calcium (see Diet). If not severe, give abrasive foods to wear it down. In more serious cases take the tortoise to the vet to have the beak cut back.

An open mouth and wheezy breathing is a sign of respiratory disease (see Respiration and Pneumonia).

The mouth can become stuck closed during hiberation. Always make sure the animal can open its mouth after hibernation. If it can't, bathe with warm water until the mucous seal is dissolved away.

The inside of the mouth can become infected, causing a yellowish growth called canker or mouth-rot. The animal won't eat, loses weight and becomes dehydrated, with a nasal discharge and a bad smell from the mouth. There is a yellowish creamy or cheesy material coating the lining of the mouth. It is predisposed by stress and an injury may start it off. It can spread from one animal to another. It is an infection caused by bacteria which usually responds to antibiotic treatment.

Take the tortoise to the vet and check accommodation and diet.

MOVEMENT

Abnormal movement in tortoises is caused by lameness or ill health (see Behaviour and Injuries).

NAILS

Animals which have free access to a normal habitat will wear their nails down. Animals kept indoors a lot, and those such as the old which take little exercise, will grow long nails that have to be cut. This is particularly so in dogs and sometimes the outer toe-nail grows round in a circle and may penetrate the pad.

Another problem is when a nail catches in a crack or crevice and tears the root attachment, causing considerable pain. The wound is liable to infection and the nail may need to be removed, so consult your vet.

The guillotine nail clippers are the best. Pincer-type nail cutters must be sharp for they squeeze the nail and can injure the quick, causing pain. The quick (sensitive tissue and blood vessels in the centre of the nail) can only be seen in non-pigmented nails so take care not to remove too much.

Cats should be provided with a scratching post of wood that doesn't splinter – a redwood log or a log to which strong carpet is attached. The cat will sharpen its claws on it and really keep them strong and clean.

Rabbits may need to have their nails cut, and budgies often do. If allowed to grow too long they may catch on the cage or perch and sprain a toe or leg.

Other small mammals seem to be trouble-free.

The nails of tortoises can get overgrown and affect its movement, and can get caught in crevices. Take the animal to the vet and have them clipped.

NAVICULAR DISEASE

A disease of a small bone called the navicular bone in the foot of the horse, usually occurring when it is between four and nine years old. It often occurs in one or both fore feet. Symptoms are lameness and stumbling which may improve during exercise.

There are several treatments, which are not always successful. Consult your vet.

NECK

Swelling of the neck in tortoises may be due to hunger oedema caused by a deficiency of protein in the diet.

A hard collar around the neck may be due to a kidney problem but it is not common.

NERVOUSNESS

Sensitivity to stress or distress.

There may be a hereditary tendency or it may be the result of a bad experience when very young. And it could be congenital, which means the animal was born that way due to a chance development but that it is not hereditary.

In all cases it can be mitigated by patient, loving handling and constant reassurance. Remember, it takes a lot of patience to build confidence and reliance, and only a few occasions of unreasonable behaviour to destroy them.

Tranquillisers have been tried but have only temporary effect. They do not effect a permanent cure.

NEUTERING

See Castration and Speying.

NIPPLE SORENESS

Not uncommon in first-time mothers. Teats are small and engorged with milk and the young can damage the teats when their teeth are sharp, in attempting to get milk.

Treatment is to wash and dry the teats at least twice a day and apply lanolin or other cream which won't affect the young one's digestion and health. Sometimes the teats need hardening (provided they are not chapped) by swabbing with methylated spirits.

NITRATES

Dangerous chemicals produced by the breakdown of decomposing food and vegetable matter in the fish tank. They are dealt with by normal bacteria and plants in what is called the nitrogen cycle of biological filtration. The decomposing material produces ammonia and nitrites which are acted upon by bacteria in the normally working tank to form nitrates which are absorbed by plants.

It is important to get your tank working properly. When you lift the lid the water should not have a bad odour.

Mechanical filtration helps to remove much of the vegetable debris, but a working tank should be the aim.

When a tank is first set up it may work well for a while and then fish die in what is called 'the new tank syndrome' because fish have been put into the tank before it has become conditioned (i.e. the nitrogen cycle is working properly), and there is a lethal rise in ammonia and nitrites. Breakdown in the nitrogen cycle can also occur if the filter stops or clogs, if too much food is given and it decomposes, or if there is not enough oxygen in the water.

The PH of the water is important. Below PH7 ammonia is less toxic. Above PH7 it becomes dangerous (see Water).

NOSE

It is normal for animals to have moist noses. Even the horse and donkey may have droplets of clear liquid in the nostrils. It is necessary for the mucous membrane of the nostrils to be moist. Any sign of drying up is abnormal and a sign of ill-health, or at least a problem.

Horses and donkeys should have a pink, moist lining to the nostril and no discharge apart from a few droplets of clear liquid.

Dogs should have moist nostrils for they lose body heat through their respiratory system, and sweat only in the paws.

Cats and other small mammals should also have damp noses for reception of smells depends on moist membranes.

Bleeding from the nose is caused by rupture of blood vessels in the nose or higher up the nasal cavity. It occurs in young horses occasionally after violent exercise. It may be due to injury, a foreign body, tumours or ulceration, or be a part of a general disease.

Discharge of pus from the nose is caused by inflammation (Rhinitis) which may be the result of injury, a foreign body, or tumours, or it may come from infected sinuses, bronchitis, pneumonia and some eye infections because drainage from the eye is into the nostril. Allergy and several general diseases such as distemper will produce a discharge.

A dry cracked nose in dogs and small mammals is a sign of

ill-health. It is wise to consult your vet for accurate diagnosis and treatment of all the above occurrences.

Discharge from a tortoise's nose can be caused by an irritant in the bedding or ground, digestive upset, the wrong environmental temperature (see Temperature), and respiratory tract or other infection. If there is no obvious cause take the animal to the vet.

NURSING

A mixture of tender loving care and applied knowledge. There is no doubt that good nursing is largely giving reassurance to your sick pet, and anticipating and ministering to its needs. A warm comfortable bed, peace and quiet, available fresh drinking water and enticing titbits to eat are essential for good nursing. Helping a house-trained animal to go out and relieve itself is sometimes overlooked and distress results. Administration of medicines and bandaging are dealt with at the end of the book.

ORPHANS

Occur when the mother dies or when she has insufficient milk. New-born young obtain colostrum (the concentrated milk produced by the mother in the first day of lactation) which contains the antibodies that protect them from disease. Their digestive system will absorb these proteins during the first 24 hours of life. An orphan that has never sucked its mother's colostrum is more difficult to raise than one that has. Your vet can inject some of these protective proteins. Subsequently it is a matter of patient, careful, frequent feeding till the orphan can drink by itself.

With horses and donkeys, fostering by another female is the simplest solution but not always available. Mothers know the smell of a strange foal so it must be disguised by rubbing it with the discharges from the womb. If that is not possible, put a strong-smelling ointment in the mare's nostrils so she cannot smell the strange foal. Tranquillisers might help during the period of introduction till the foal is accepted.

If fostering is not possible, foals are best fed from a bottle with a teat of the correct size which can be bought from horse and farm suppliers. A wide range of milk substitutes are available with instructions how to make up and feed and they should be followed accurately. As a rough guide the foal should be given about 1 litre (1.7 pints) of liquid milk substitute for each 10 kg. (22 lbs) body weight per day, separated into at least four feeds. Increase this amount as the foal grows, giving it as much as it will take readily at each feed.

Puppies and kittens are much easier to foster if a lactating mother can be found. She will usually readily accept the orphan. If this is not possible, substitute milk is available and is much preferred to cow's milk which can cause serious digestive upset. Again follow the instructions carefully. Feed every 3 hours to begin with, using an eye-dropper at first and later a bottle with a teat. It is important to keep the orphans warm at roughly body heat (36°–38°C or 96°–100°F) as far as possible, and a blanket-lined box near the hot water tank may work. But take care it is not hotter than this.

Orphan rabbits, rats and guinea pigs can be reared in the same way, using an eye-dropper to feed the milk. Later a bottle with a small teat or a small medicine bottle may work.

Hamsters are much more difficult and orphans rarely survive long enough after their mother's death to be fed successfully,

PADS
Susceptible to injury from thorns, broken glass, etc. A cut pad will bleed profusely but dressed and bandaged properly it will heal quickly.

Dry, cracked pads are a sign of illness and a vet should be consulted.

In dogs cysts can develop between the pads. They are very painful and infected. Bathing in Epsom salts solution (1 dessertspoon to ½ pint of hot water) may bring the cyst to a head and draw out the pus contents. Antibiotic therapy will help. If the cysts recur a vaccine can be made from a swab of the pus with a good chance of success.

PAIN
Nature's way of teaching us what is harmful and also encouraging us to rest, or at least to rest the painful part, because rest aids healing.

It is the owner's job to investigate the cause of the pain and assist in the healing when possible. Pain is a valuable aid in diagnosis, for usually it pinpoints the affected part or organ.

Referred pain presents a problem – a pain in the arm could be from the heart, a pain on the point of the shoulder from the chest cavity, and a pain in the back from the kidneys.

Unless the pain is severe it is not wise to give the animal pain-killers for it doesn't understand it must rest. Only pain tells it that.

Tortoises have the physiological capacity to feel pain but it is not easy to diagnose. Severe pain can cause loss of appetite.

It has been proved conclusively that fish possess the same nerve pathways and receptors as man through which he senses pain. It can be concluded therefore that fish can feel pain. The transparent thin membrane covering fish is very sensitive, as is the area around the mouth.

PAINT REMOVAL

Water-soluble paint is harmless and will wash or wear off quickly. Oil paint contains white spirit which is irritant to the skin. If the paint is on the ends of the hairs of the coat it can be combed out with patience. Paint on the skin, especially the feet, can cause inflammation and is best removed using white spirit, but immediately afterwards wash thoroughly with a shampoo to remove all the spirit. Then dry and apply lanolin or zinc ointment.

PARALYSIS

Caused by damage to the nerves supplying the paralysed part. This can be due to injury, haemorrhage, an abscess close to the nerve, or a slipped disc pressing on the spinal cord. It can also be caused by hip dysplasia, fracture of the pelvis and ruptured ligaments.

Some diseases like distemper in dogs, tetanus, and encephalitis can cause general paralysis, as can lead poisoning and aortic thrombosis.

Treatment depends on the cause and expert veterinary help is required.

PARASITES

Creatures living on (ectoparasites) or inside (endoparasites) the animal.

They are dealt with under specific headings – fleas, lice, mites, ticks, worms and coccidia.

Tortoises can become infested with ectoparasites (see Ticks and Mites) and worms (see Worms) and protozoa (see Enteritis, Protozoa and Amoebic Infestation).

PARVO

An abbreviation of Canine Parvo Virus infection, a virus disease of dogs causing sudden death in young pups following increased heart and respiratory rates, fatigue and collapse. Older pups and adults are depressed, refusing food, and often vomit and have diarrhoea coupled with fatigue and fast heart and respiratory rates. Many die.

Take the dog to the vet at once for diagnosis and treatment. A good vaccine is available (see Vaccination).

PENIS

See Injuries for tortoises.

PERITONITIS

Inflammation of the inside of the abdomen, caused usually by injury or rupture of the intestines, or associated with a generalised infection.

In cats there is a special disease called feline infectious peritonitis where it is a primary condition.

In the horse severe colic can cause peritonitis, especially if the intestines are damaged by migrating worm larvae, or torsion of the bowel, or a puncture wound or ulceration.

In the puppy severe enteritis by itself can cause the condition or cause telescoping of the bowel which is followed by peritonitis. Bowel obstruction can cause it.

In birds peritonitis can occur when a bird becomes eggbound and it certainly will result if the egg is broken inside the bird.

Symptoms are acute pain, swelling of the abdomen, loss of appetite and fever, and some cases may vomit. Seek veterinary help at once.

PHARYNGITIS

Inflammation of the pharynx (back of the throat). It can be caused by respiratory disease, some other bacterial or virus infection, tonsillitis, swallowing irritants, or a foreign body stuck in the throat or causing injury while being swallowed. The animal may go off its food and cough. If severe, it may retch and breathe faster than normal.

Treatment depends on the cause. Antibiotics and medicine to soothe the inflamed lining of the throat are indicated. It is best to consult your vet.

PLANTS

Not only serve as decoration and provide fish with a more interesting and varied environment, but they also play a part in the nitrogen cycle. There are a great many available. Some are fast-growing, others grow very slowly. Advice should be sought from a good supplier. Perhaps the commonest plant used for its appearance and as a good oxygenator is Vallisnavia Spiralis.

The most important thing to remember is that plants can carry parasites and disease. Obtain them from a reputable, established supplier and establish the plant in a separate tank with perhaps one or two fish before establishing it in your fish tank. Alternatively, sterilise the plants with potassium permanganate made up to a dark red solution (the supplier will tell you what the plants can stand). Take care to rinse the permanagate off the plants with clean water before putting them in your tank.

PLASTRON

The underneath part of the shell of a tortoise (see Shell).

PLEURISY

Inflammation of the lining of the chest cavity and the membrane covering the lungs. It is usually the result of an infection though it can result from a puncture wound of the chest, or rupture of the lung, or cancer. Sometimes the inflammation is accompanied by effusion of fluid which compresses the lungs, making breathing more difficult, and compresses the heart, which interferes with blood circulation.

Symptoms are decreased appetite, fever, and pain in the chest. If fluid forms, there will be difficulty in breathing, breathlessness and lethargy with possibly bluish gums and other mucous membranes. Consult the vet.

PNEUMONIA

Inflammation of the lungs. Usually it is a broncho-pneumonia with both bronchi and lungs inflamed.

It can be caused by infection with a virus, bacterium or fungus, or worm larvae migrating through the lung tissue. It can follow infection of the upper respiratory tract or be caused by inhalation of fluid or solids, which sometimes occurs after vomiting while the animal is unconscious. Respiratory viruses are the most common causes.

Symptoms are decreased appetite, fever, increased rate of respiration, pain in the chest, some coughing and a nasal discharge. Later there may be heart problems.

Treatment depends on the cause – antibiotics, cough remedies, rest, warmth, and sometimes cortico-steroids. Consult your vet. For some of the major virus diseases there are effective vaccines (see Vaccination).

Pneumonia in tortoises causes loss of appetite, apathy, and wheezy respiratory sounds. The causes are viruses, bacteria, fungi, and very occasionally, the larvae of certain worms. It is necessary to take the tortoise to the vet for diagnosis and treatment.

POISONING

Animals are susceptible to a number of poisons. Only common ones are dealt with here, and poisoning with drugs only available on prescription is excluded.

Horses and donkeys and other herbivorous animals can be poisoned by spoilt food where some decomposition and contamination with bacteria have taken place. More common vegetable poisons are:

Alphatoxin, causing loss of appetite, dullness, indigestion and possibly enteritis, and possibly jaundice and death. There is no specific antidote.

Bracken, which causes incoordination of movement: later muscle tremors appear, with slowing and irregularity of the heart. Later the animal may collapse and heart rate becomes fast. Treatment is injections of thiamine if caught early. Separate animal from bracken.

Caster oil beans are very poisonous though symptoms may take two days to develop. They cause enteritis with dullness and incoordination. Later sweating and a very powerful heartbeat and diarrhoea. Treatment as for Shock.

Hemlock, which grows along banks of streams. It is very poisonous, causing weakness, staggering, dilating pupils and laboured respiration. Treatment is to remove poison with purgatives.

Horsetail Symptoms are similar to bracken poisoning. Treat with thiamine by mouth.

Laburnum is very poisonous. All parts are dangerous. The horse is most susceptible. Symptoms are excitement, then incoordination, sweating, and later convulsions and asphyxia. Treatment is symptomatic till poison clears.

Moulds A variety are involved, growing on damp hay and other food. They can cause a variety of symptoms from liver damage to eczema. Generally there is loss of appetite, depression, weakness, and sometimes death. There is no specific treatment.

Ragwort is poisonous both when fresh and when dried in hay. The latter form is more dangerous because the animal cannot avoid eating it. It is a chronic poison affecting the liver, causing dullness, a rapid pulse and respiration, loss of condition and weakness. Colic may occur and jaundice may develop days or weeks later. There is no specific treatment. Methionine has been recommended.

Deadly Nightshade and Thorn Apples release atropine when eaten. It is very poisonous, causing dilation of the pupils, impaired vision, loss of appetite and muscular spasms, and a rapid and high death rate. Treatment consists of purgatives and stimulants.

Yew Tree is the most deadly plant poison in Britain and only a small amount can cause rapid death, perhaps while the animal is still eating it, with no struggling. Symptoms, which are not often seen, are trembling, difficult respiration and collapse. All parts of the tree are dangerous, whether green or dried. There is no treatment.

Poisoning with chemicals can affect both herbivorous and carnivorous animals:

Arsenic is one of the two most common poisons affecting animals (the other is lead). It is a cumulative poison used in agricultural foot baths and horticulture, and it does not have a repellent taste. Symptoms are intense pain in the abdomen, staggering, collapse and paralysis, and the passage of blood in the urine.

Herbicides and Insecticides are all highly poisonous – acute poisoning from a large dose causes apprehension and a change of behaviour, then muscle spasms, salivation and chewing and champing of the jaws which causes frothing. The animal stumbles and walks aimlessly, later grinds its teeth and has groaning convulsions and finally dies. Less acute symptoms are much the same but milder and without convulsions or muscle tremors. Abnormal behaviour and gait may be all there is to see.

Lead in the form of lead paint seems to be attractive to some animals and it is an accumulative poison. Poisoning can occur from drinking water containing lead (dissolved by soft water containing nitrates) and there are many other sources.

Acute lead poisoning is rarely seen in pets. Chronic poisoning occurs in dogs and horses and occasionally in other animals. Symptoms are loss of weight, gradual paralysis, swelling of the knees and a blue-black discoloration of the gums. In dogs and cats, in addition, anaemia develops.

Lead poisoning is not uncommon in water birds. The population of swans on the Thames has been reduced by poisoning with lead shot and anglers' weights.

There is a specific antidote so consult your vet.

Mercury is used to dress agricultural seed and is sometimes eaten by horses. Ointments containing mercury can be absorbed by cats and dogs and poison them. Symptoms are gastro-enteritis and diarrhoea followed by shock and death. If less acute, the kidneys are damaged, resulting in nephritis (see Nephritis).

Rat poisons may accidentally be eaten by dogs and other small mammals. There are many different types. The corrosive type causes gastro-enteritis and the Warfarin type causes haemorrhages at various sites in the body. There is only treatment for Warfarin, namely Vitamin K injection.

Slug killer (metaldehyde) has poisoned cats and dogs. Symptoms are incoordination, increased heart and breathing rates, and later loss of consciousness and cyanosis (lack of oxygen). There is no specific treatment. Give an emetic to empty stomach of any that hasn't been absorbed. Stimulants will help. Consult your vet.

Tortoises are susceptible to poisoning from insecticides which they get from food that has been sprayed, and from eating poisonous plants. But if a correct diet is offered this should not happen. Take the animal to your vet if you suspect poisoning.

Fish are very susceptible to poisoning. Nitrites, ammonia and nitrates are toxic (see Nitrites). Tobacco smoke and paint fumes can be toxic if concentrations are high, and especially if an aeration pump is bubbling air into the tank. Aerosol insecticides are dangerous and highly chlorinated water is not recommended for filling tanks. Prolonged contact with plastic and plasticisers used to keep hosepipes supple can poison fish.

Remember that certain treatments like phenoxythol can release toxins from the activated carbon filter and poison the fish. Methylene blue may stop the nitrogen cycle causing a build up of nitrites.

If the PH of the water is too high, free ammonia is formed which is poisonous and causes symptoms of suffocation. The fish breathes irregularly and with difficulty and snaps for air at the water surface. Reduce the PH by careful addition of acid. Move the fish to clean water.

An excess of carbon dioxide is also poisonous, causing similar symptoms of oxygen lack. Carbon dioxide can only accumulate if PH is low.

When water conditions are not correct the fish may dart about or even jump out of the water (see Water).

POULTICE

A method of applying heat to an area. Mainly used to mature an abscess. There are special products on the market but bread will also work. The area is covered with sterile gauze and the hot poultice is placed on top and bandaged to keep it there. A poultice ½ inch (12 mm.) thick will retain heat long enough to have some effect. Test the heat with your fingers to make sure it is not too hot. Renew several times during the day.

PREGNANCY

Periods of pregnancy (called gestation periods) are as follows:

Horses	11 months
Donkeys	11 months
Dogs	63 days
Cats	63 days
Rabbits	30–32 days
Guinea-pigs	68 days
Hamsters	18–21 days
Gerbils	18–21 days
Rats	18–21 days

False pregnancy can occur due to a hormone imbalance. The female shows behavioural signs of being pregnant and may even produce milk at the correct time after the heat when mating would have taken place. It can be corrected by hormone therapy. Consult your vet.

PROLAPSE

The extrusion of the rectum (rectal prolapse) or the vagina or uterus, usually after giving birth, though it can occur while the animal is heavily pregnant.

Rectal prolapse is normally caused by severe enteritis accompanied by straining. Occasionally in dogs on a diet containing a lot of bones, the faeces are hard and dry and cause prolapse because of excessive straining.

Straining whilst giving birth is the cause of vaginal or uterine prolapse, especially if the afterbirth does not detach normally.

PROTOZOA

A number of protozoa species can affect tortoises and affect mainly the digestive and urinary tracts.

Treatment for some is available. Consult your vet.

PULSE

Can be felt in horses and donkeys inside the front leg high up between the chest and the leg. In dogs and cats it is felt on the inside of the hind leg. In rabbits it may be felt in the ear artery. In smaller animals the same site as in the dog may be tried but the heart rate is fast and the animal not prepared to remain still. The rate and character tell the vet about the blood circulation.

PYOMETRA

The name for pus in the uterus. It is not uncommon in dogs, less common in cats and rare in other animals. It occurs in animals over five years old as a rule and is caused by an imbalance of hormones occurring after heat.

Symptoms are dullness, thirst, loss of appetite and swelling of the abdomen. The animal passes a lot of urine and may vomit occasionally. There may or may not be a discharge from the vulva.

The best treatment is surgical removal of the uterus. Consult your vet (See also Uterus).

QUARANTINE

The isolation of an introduced animal for a long enough period for symptoms of disease to develop. The purpose is to make sure disease is not brought in accidentally. Britain is one of the few countries free of rabies, a deadly disease for animals and humans. So the law demands six months' quarantine in licensed kennels – that being more than the incubation period.

There are many more diseases animals can carry and it is wise to isolate a new animal for at least two weeks which is the incubation time for most diseases. In addition, a veterinary examination is advisable just before you put the new animal with the others.

Quarantine for both plants and fish is essential once a working, balanced tank is set up. It should be combined with sterilisation for plants (see Plants), but for fish this is not possible, so a fish should be kept on its own to see if any problems develop before being introduced into an established tank. A period of at least two weeks is advisable.

RABIES

A virus disease of the nervous system that can infect all mammals, including man, who will die a horrible death if not treated in time.

It is spread by the saliva of animals in the terminal stages which contaminates a wound on another animal; in other words, it is usually spread by infected animals biting others. The incubation period can be as short as 10 days or as long as 6 months – hence the quarantine period of 6 months which has kept rabies out of the British Isles. Because of this measure no person need fear rabies when bitten by an animal in the UK. In other countries there is always a grave risk, and a course of 13 painful preventative injections, which are themselves risky, *must* be started at once.

There is a good animal vaccine available, but because we do not have rabies in the UK its use is not allowed, nor is it necessary. It may be given to dogs which are just about to be exported, but approval must first be obtained from the Ministry of Agriculture, Fisheries and Food.

Attempts to smuggle animals into the UK carry stiff penalties.

RESPIRATION

In tortoises cannot be accomplished by expanding the ribs because of the fixed immovable shell. Air is drawn in by means of moving the abdominal contents and creating negative pressure to draw in air.

Tortoises can produce hissing sounds by expelling air forcefully.

For respiration in fish, see Gills.

RESTRAINT

Resolute, quiet confidence is the major part of successful restraint. An animal knows when it must submit.

For horses and donkeys a halter or bridle may be all that is needed. To examine the hind feet and quarters, get someone to hold up a fore foot, with the animal alongside a bare wall to restrict its movements. When examining teeth or dosing by mouth, holding an ear, as well as the halter, is usually sufficient.

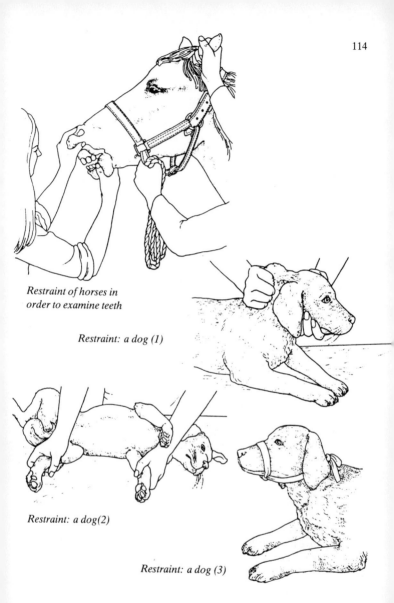

Restraint of horses in order to examine teeth

Restraint: a dog (1)

Restraint: a dog(2)

Restraint: a dog (3)

In the donkey, grasping a fold of skin over the shoulder is better than trying to hold an ear, which some donkeys resent. A twitch should not be used.

If the animal is in pain and is particularly difficult to handle, your vet can inject sedatives and tranquillisers.

Dogs may be restrained for examination and treatment by firmly grasping the scruff of the neck. Or place the animal on its side on a table, and with the dog's back to you, lean over and grasp the underneath legs and lean your elbows and forearms on the animal's body. If the dog tends to bite, a bandage can be tied round its jaws to keep the mouth closed. Liquid medicines can still be given via the cheek pouch.

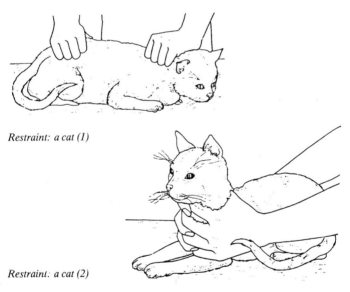

Restraint: a cat (1)

Restraint: a cat (2)

Cats are restrained by firmly grasping the scruff, and if it still struggles, holding both hind legs in the other hand. To open the mouth, take a firm grip of the scruff and bend the head backwards and the mouth will open and the lower jaw become slack.

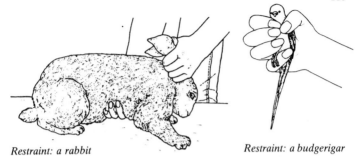

Restraint: a rabbit   *Restraint: a budgerigar*

The ears of rabbits can be grasped only if the animal's body is supported in the hand or on a table. Its back legs are strong and its nails can damage your skin.

Rats are held by the base of their tails. Guinea pigs are held firmly by a hand on each side of the body. Hamsters and gerbils are also held in the hands.

Birds are held in a cupped hand with the legs between your second and third fingers, and the tail and flight feathers stretching back between your thumb and first finger. Hold firmly but not tight. If a bird feels itself loose it will struggle.

Handling of tortoises should only be done when necessary and all movements should be slow to minimise stress. They may urinate or defecate when handled. Take great care not to drop them, for this may cause serious injury. Don't hold head or limbs out as this will interfere with breathing. Don't turn the tortoise on its back nor rotate it rapidly. Wait until it puts its head out if you want to examine that region. Remember it can bite.

Fish should not be handled unless absolutely necessary. To examine a fish, isolate it in a jar of clean water. Samples of diseased tissue can be taken by holding the fish with a plastic glove or bag. Do not handle fish with bare hands as this will damage its skin.

RICKETS

An abnormality of the ends or epiphyses of the bones of growing animals caused by a deficiency of minerals and vitamin D.

It is unlikely to be seen in horses and donkeys nowadays as

manufactured diets include supplements.

It is not uncommon in dogs, especially the large breeds, for the growth rate of the puppy is more rapid and even a slight deficiency in the diet will result in rickets. The first signs are swelling of the ends of the limb bones and the ends of the ribs where they join the cartilege of the bottom of the chest, two-thirds of the way down the side of the chest. Later, lameness and bending of the limb bones may occur.

Cats and smaller animal don't often suffer from rickets.

Treatment is to give adequate minerals, particularly calcium and phosporous and vitamin D, in the diet. However, if it is deficient in these, other vitamins and minerals may also be lacking so it is wise to review the diet (see Diet).

RIG

Describes a male horse that has a testicle retained in the abdomen, where because of the slightly higher temperature it does not develop normally.

The hormones it produces often make the animal unpredictable. It will try to mate with females and cause problems.

Treatment is an operation to remove the abnormal testicle. Consult your vet. There is a blood test available.

RINGWORM

A fungus that infects the skin and is spread by direct or indirect contact.

Horses and donkeys can get five different types, but one of these is by far the most common, and young thin-skinned animals are the most susceptible. The fungus takes hold when there is very superficial injury such as a girth rub.

Symptoms are loss of hair and inflammation spreading in a roughly circular fashion. The infection can be on any part of the body but most usually in the saddle and girth regions.

In most cases the animal develops an immunity and the ringworm regresses and may disappear. There are effective treatments, one taken internally and several applied externally, and the manufacturer's instructions should be followed carefully. The spores of the fungus get on to brushes and combs, saddles and the walls of the stable or box. They are very resistant and will live for months. It is necessary to wash and disinfect carefully and thoroughly.

Dogs get a different species of ringworm which causes round lesions with raised edges. Hair may not all be lost. Parts most affected are head, feet and legs. Treatment as for horses (see above.)

Cats may only have a dull coat and itchiness, and perhaps a few broken hairs. But it sheds dandruff resembling cigarette ash on the coat. Treatment as for horses.

Other small animals can get ringworm but it is uncommon.

It is important to remember that all species of ringworm can infect humans.

SANDCRACK

A vertical crack in the wall of the hoof of horses and donkeys. It either begins at the bottom and splits upwards or begins at the coronet. The condition is caused by injury to the cells at the coronet from which the horny wall grows.

Cracks from the bottom are due to improper care of the foot, neglecting regular trimming or bad shoeing.

Treatment consists of cutting a transverse groove across the top of the crack. It should be as deep as possible without drawing blood. Also the farrier should trim the foot and shoe it properly.

If the crack is very deep there may be bleeding and even pus. Call the vet at once.

SCALDS
See Burns.

SCRATCHING

May be simply self-grooming to clear the skin of shed hair and debris.

Excessive scratching is a sign that there may be ectoparasites, or infection of the skin, or allergy. And sometimes the animal is so persistent and vigorous that the skin is damaged.

It is best to consult your vet.

SEDATIVES

Rarely required for animals. The simplest and best method is to put the animal in a snug box or house that is peaceful and quiet and devoid of distraction, because animals do not appear to have circling thoughts like humans.

Should for any reason a sedative be required it is best to consult your vet, as there may be a pathological problem that needs to be diagnosed. Unless it is absolutely necessary it is not wise to give animals sedatives before being transported as horses and donkeys may collapse and injure themselves, and other animals may become so depressed they don't breathe properly, and when ventilation is poor this could lead to shock or death.

Professional advice should be sought.

SEPTICAEMIA

A form of blood poisoning with bacteria that follows infection, somewhere else – a bad wound infection, mastitis, pneumonia, and infection of the uterus after giving birth are examples. It is very serious and before antibiotics were available it often caused death.

Symptoms are severe depression, no appetite, fever progressing to shock. Consult your vet at once.

SEXING

Male tortoises generally have a longer and thicker tail and the shell is concave on the underside (the plastron). Females have a flat underside and a short tail about one inch (25 mm.) long. In general the cloaca of the female is nearer to the root of the tail than in the male.

It is not possible to sex young immature animals.

Regarding birds, consult your vet.

SEXUAL FRUSTRATION

In tortoises can occur where there are two or more males and no females, though it can occur in a solitary male.

They become hyperactive, aggressive, refuse to feed and attempt to mount objects. There will be intermittent periods of lethargy.

Providing a larger, more interesting enclosure will help.

SHAMPOOING
See Washing.

SHELL

The tortoise's shell consists of two parts, the dome-shaped top called the carapace, and the flatter underneath part called the plastron. The shell is composed of scales of keratin like the human nail, and bony plates underneath to which the main portion of the spine is attached. The numbers and borders of scales do not correspond to the bony plates underneath.

The shell is soft in hatchlings and gradually becomes hard and unyielding in the first year or so. Abnormal conditions affecting the shell are: deformities usually due to wrong diet, injuries, and diseases.

Softening of the shell allowing indentations to be made is due to a nutritional imbalance of calcium and phosphorus in the diet. Uneven growth of the shell with plates raised and an unnaturally high dome, white growth rings, and ridges between plates of plastron is also nutritional, with too much or too little protein in the diet and insufficient exercise. Certain deformities of the shell restrict leg movement causing an abnormal walking gait.

Cracks in the shell are caused by falling on a hard surface. If the crack has dirt in it, or is more than a hair's breadth, take the tortoise to the vet for treatment. A transverse line across the plastron is not necessarily a fracture in some species. Scratches on the plastron result from sharp rocks in the pen. They should be removed.

Discoloration of the plastron – patches of yellow, orange or brown, and areas of flaking scales with the pink tissue underneath perhaps exposed – is caused by the floor being too damp, or it may be dietary, or an infection. Bathe the area in weak potassium permanganate solution once daily for two or three days. If the scutes (scales) are separating and there appears to be suppuration, the cause could be burns from heating appliances. Careful attention to the wound is required or it can become infected with fly larvae. Gently remove loose scutes and carefully clean the area. It is better to call the vet.

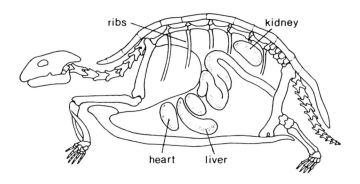

Anatomy of a tortoise

Inflammation from bacterial infection can be treated with certain antibiotics such as neomysin and nystatin. Such infections are loosely called Shell Rot. Take the animal to the vet for accurate diagnosis and treatment.

In older tortoises the scales may begin to flake off. Check the diet. Nutrition may be faulty (see Diet).

SHOCK

Caused by failure of the circulation of the blood, which in turn affects several organs. It can be caused by severe haemorrhage, bad burns, serious accidents, severe gastro-enteritis, septicaemia, toxaemia (blood poisoning with toxins), snake-bite poison, heart failure, and the terminal stages of any diseases. It can also be an allergic reaction and it can be caused by severe stress to the nervous system.

Symptoms are weakness followed by collapse, no attempt to move, subnormal body temperature with cold extremities, and a rapid heartbeat and weak pulse. The pupils become dilated.

Treatment is aimed at improving blood circulation and this depends on the cause. Immediate veterinary help is essential.

Tortoises are susceptible to shock due to being dropped or

serious injury. Keep the animal in a quiet dark place at the correct temperature until it has recovered.

Fish are subject to shock, which often results in death or disease. The fish becomes sluggish or almost motionless and is disinclined to move. Watch for signs of disease and be ready to isolate in a clean tank of water.

SHOEING

Of horses and donkeys is done to prevent wear of the hoof which would otherwise be excessive on hard road. It is not necessary when animals are kept in fields or soft ground.

It is a job for an expert and a qualified or skilled farrier should be employed. Shoes must be made to fit the feet, and not the feet cut to fit the shoe. Because of the growth rate of the hoof shoes must be removed, the feet trimmed and the animal reshod every six weeks.

Special types of shoes are available to correct some limb and posture problems.

SINUSITIS

Inflammation of the facial sinuses (air cavities in the facial structure) which are lined with mucous membranes. It can be caused by bacterial or fungus infection, or associated with respiratory disease, also abscesses spreading from diseased molar teeth, and cancer.

Symptoms are sneezing, head shaking and discharge from the nose. For proper diagnosis and treatment your vet should be consulted.

SKIN

The envelope containing the body is a most important structure. It provides protection and regulates the body temperature. It is subject to injury, infection, allergic reactions and cancer.

Injury can be bruising which damages some of the cells and causes small haemorrhages followed by swelling (see Bruises), or wounds (see Wounds), or burns (see Burns).

Infection can be with bacteria (Dermatitis), fungus (see Ringworm), or mites (see Mange). Bacterial infections begin where there has been injury (insect bites, bruising, wounds, burns, or friction between folds of skin).

Cancer can be in the form of warts, or of rodent ulcers, or skin tumours. Normally they can be removed by a veterinary surgeon. Symptoms are swelling, reddening heat in the area, and later, oozing and crusting and scaling with loss of hair.

Acne is infection of the glands of the skin causing small pustules at each site.

Eczema (see Eczema) is a name given to types of dermatitis, including allergic dermatitis which is caused by sensitivity to an item of diet or, in the horse, sensitivity to fly bites. Another cause in dogs and cats is impacted anal glands which normally empty daily. Instead the poisonous material is absorbed to circulate in the blood and often causes eczema.

Treatments depend on the cause and it is wisest to consult a vet.

Rubbed or scratched skin of tortoises where some scales have been lost may be due to inappropriate fencing or sharp stones etc. in the compound. Skin may be injured or infected and have ectoparasites present (see Injuries, Dermatitis, Ticks and Mange).

In fish, below the thin transparent layer there are scales and lots of mucous cells which secrete a thick slimy mucus that acts as a lubricant to reduce friction with the water and protects against disease. It also assists in the water balance or osmo regulation of the fish to keep its body fluids constant. The horny scales grow from under the skin and act as a support and a protective layer.

There are a number of diseases affecting the skin, some of which affect the colour of the fish. Paleness may be a sign of tuberculosis. Dark colouration may be caused by some skin diseases and tumours. Often skin disease causes irritation and the fish may rub itself on rocks and plants, especially if infected with parasites, and the slime (mucus) secretion increases.

Fungal diseases of the skin are very common. The spores of the fungus are present in nearly every tank but don't cause disease unless the skin is injured. For treatment it is not necessary to distinguish the exact fungus. It is seen as fine white or off-white threads and may even resemble cotton wool if infection is severe.

Remove infected fish from the tank and paint the affected area with weak iodine or 1% mercurochrome or 1% malachite green and place the fish in water containing 1 ml. of standard 1% B.P. methylene blue solution in 4.5 litres (1 gallon) of water. The colour of the water will gradually fade. Repeat if necessary to kill the fungal infection.

White Spot or Ichthyophthiriasis is also a common infection. It is caused by a protozoon (a single-celled parasite) which penetrates the skin and causes white or grey spots all over the body surface and fins. It feeds on blood and skin cells. Each adult can produce 1,000 or so young which soon die if they can't infect another fish. So a tank left empty will become safe in three weeks or so. Treatment is not easy for the parasite is buried in the fish and protected from medication. It is necessary to expose the fish to treated water for a longer period so that the parasite is killed when it leaves the fish. Medicate the water with 1 ml. of 1% methylene blue solution B.P. in 4½ litres of water (1 gallon) and repeat after three days when the colour of the water will have faded.

Pox Disease is also widespread. It is caused by a virus which causes raised white spots which may coalesce into patches. The fish will usually recover and there is no treatment.

Velvet or Rust Disease is characterised by a pale yellow 'dust' which covers the skin. It is also caused by a parasite – a protozoon. It can also be treated with methylene blue as described for White Spot.

Chilodnelliasis causes slimy skin and gills. It is a bacterial infection that is treated with the same methylene blue treatment as described for White Spot.

Black Spot is caused by the larval stage of a worm that infects water birds. Each black spot contains the encysted larva. They occur all over the skins, fins, even the eye and mouth. Fish are the intermediate hosts. Treatment consists of bathing the fish in a 1 in 20,000 solution of picric acid for one hour.

SLIPPED DISC

The extrusion of a cartilage-like disc from where it normally lies between the vertebrae to the lumen of the spinal canal where it presses on the spinal cord. It normally occurs in the lower lumbar vertebrae. It is not uncommon in dogs, less common in horses and cats, and rare if ever in smaller pets.

Symptoms are pain and stiffness of the back. If the pressure of the spinal cord is greater, partial paralysis of the hind limbs can occur.

Treatment is manipulation by experienced people which can sometimes get it back. Otherwise pain-killers are prescribed. Once partial paralysis has occurred only an operation can help.

SNEEZING

Which occurs in all animals, is a reflex action to get rid of irritation in the nostrils which can be caused by dust particles, foreign bodies like a grass awn, bleeding or pus coming down from the nose, infection, tumours, and an allergy.

If sneezing continues it is best to consult your vet.

SPEYING

Removing the ovaries and sometimes the uterus as well to stop the animal breeding, but more important to stop it coming on heat and to avoid the behavioural changes which accompany heat (see Heat).

It is necessary to open the abdomen and an anaesthetic is required, which means a vet. The operation is best done when the animal is young.

Mares and jennys are rarely speyed and they can be done at any age.

Bitches are best operated on before they are a year old. Some bitches may put on weight afterwards and become lethargic.

Cats are best done about five months of age. They are less likely to become lazy and fat.

Small animals are not often speyed.

SPRAIN

A tear of a ligament which supports a joint, for example in the limbs. An awkward slip or wrench of the joint can cause a sprain.

Symptoms are pain (lameness if in a limb), swelling and heat in the area.

Treatment consists of giving support by bandaging and rest. There are solutions and injections to reduce the inflammation and ointments to increase blood supply to the part to aid healing. Consult your vet.

STAGGERING

Can be caused by a variety of conditions such as serious disease,
shock, heart attack, anaemia, diabetes, eclampsia (blood calcium
deficiency), debilitating disease and emaciation, tetanus and
encephalitis, and injury and disease of the spinal cord and blood
and nerve supply of the hind limbs.

Treatment depends on accurate diagnosis and that is a job for the
vet.

STINGS

In Britain only wasps and bees are of any significance. Spiders, ants
and other biting and stinging insects, apart from parasites, are only
a nuisance.

Wasp and bee stings can hurt and startle the animal, and if it is
sensitive the sting could trigger off an allergic response. Bees inject
an acid irritant and wasps an alkaline one that causes swelling, pain
and inflammation. Not infrequently dogs and cats get stung the
mouth. Watch carefully in case the swelling is at the back of the
mouth or tongue and interferes with breathing.

Treatment: baking soda rubbed into the sting aperture will help
to neutralise the venom. Antihistamine cream will be useful and if
the reaction is severe antihistamine tablets or injections can be
given. Normally the pain and swelling will recede in a few hours.

Occasionally horses, donkeys and dogs get bitten by an adder.
Considerable swelling results but pain is not excessive. Treatment,
if animal is found when bitten, is to wash out the poison. Keep quiet
and still to reduce speed of absorption and circulation of venom.
Watch for bad reaction and call your vet for help.

STOMACH

Acts as a receptacle for food, and is where digestion begins.
Inflammation can be caused by irritant substances that have been
swallowed, or that are produced by the decomposition of decaying
and contaminated food; and also by infection. Apart from
discomfort and pain, inflammation may cause vomiting – see
Gastritis.

STRAIN

Applies to damage to tendons, which are the structures that join muscles to bones at a distance. Most tendons are in the limbs. Damage is caused by overstretching or awkward, sudden movement. The typical example is strain of the tendons of the limbs of the horse, often caused by jumping and landing heavily and awkwardly.

Treatment consists of rest and supportive bandages. There are solutions to apply and injections to give to reduce inflammation, and ointment to improve the blood supply to the part.

STRESS

The mechanisms of the body's reaction to stimuli (stressors). It is also a collective name for the stimuli and hence a lot of confusion over terminology. The animal avoids too little stimulus because of monotony, and too much is avoided whenever possible. But if it cannot be avoided and the stimulus is abnormal and/or extreme, a point is reached when the protective mechanisms can no longer cope and pathological symptoms develop, the defence system begins to fail, and susceptibility to disease increases.

The mechanism is complex. There is production of corticosteroids, which affect many organs, and changes in the brain's chemistry and the functioning of other organs.

Causes of abnormal stress are psychological, such as confinement in ususual surroundings that cause apprehension, continual frightening circumstances such as dominance, fighting, being chased, and being cruelly treated. Physical factors are: enforced work (horses, donkeys and dogs), injuries that are very painful, burns, diseases, and prolonged exposure to very cold conditions.

Treatment for excessive stress is rest and quiet for a prolonged period and supplements of vitamin C in the diet, which must be enticing, balanced and given regularly.

Tortoises are subject to stress due to wrong diet, inappropriate accommodation, frequent handling, and temperatures outside the required range. Stress may make the animal prone to disease.

Fish are susceptible to stress, which is often followed by disease. It is important to quarantine newly purchased fish for three weeks before introducing them to your tank.

There are no vaccines available to protect fish so the only way to keep them healthy is to provide a good environment and avoid introducing parasites or diseases with new fish or live food on plants.

SWELLINGS

Can be caused by inflammation, for example, abscesses, sprains, strains, internal bleeding, stings, allergic reactions, tumours and cancer, mastitis, hernias, and bony growths resulting from injury or disease.

Diagnosis depends on site of swelling and its character, that is, whether painful, hot, soft or hard, and any other symptoms.

Swelling of the abdomen may be wind, faeces, fluid, pregnancy, or tumours.

Swelling of: the ear is probably a haematoma
the eyes is probably an allergic reaction
the face is probably an allergic condition or an abscessed upper molar tooth
the lip is probably a result of a sting or allergy
the naval is probably a hernia
the groin is probably a hernia
the joints is probably arthritis or bony growth
the mammary gland is probably mastitis
the vulva is probably heat

TANK

Fish should not be kept in a fish bowl or empty container devoid of plants and other natural living things. Though their brains are small they can suffer. A proper ecologically balanced community should be the aim. It is aesthetically pleasing and fulfils the biological needs of the fish.

The size depends on the situation of the tank. It must be placed where it receives enough light to allow plants to grow, and away from strong sunlight which could overheat the water in the summer. It must not be in a cold draught which could overcool the water, and it must not be placed where it can be knocked as it is vulnerable to breakage.

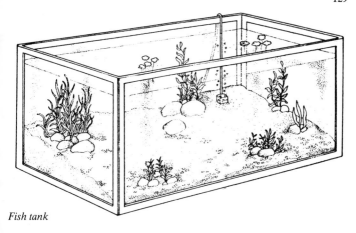

Fish tank

But of course plants will grow in artificial light, which must be on for about eight hours each day. Too long a duration of light can cause overgrowth of the plants.

The number of fish the tank can accommodate depends on the surface area of the water, where oxygen is dissolved. Calculate the surface area in square inches and divide by 13 to give the maximum number of small fish; divide by 18 for the number of medium-sized fish; by 20 for large fish (3 or 4 inches, or 7.6–10 cm. long); and by 30 for small goldfish. So a tank 2 feet long by 18 inches wide (i.e., 610 × 457 cm.) will have a surface area of 432 square inches and can hold 33 small fish or 14 small goldfish.

Your newly purchased tank should be thoroughly rinsed out with clean water. If it has been used before it should first be disinfected and then rinsed out. Place it in position and begin to place in position rocks and gravel that have been thoroughly washed, disinfected or boiled, and rinsed with about a dozen water changes. The gravel should be about 2 inches (5 cm.) deep on the bottom. Don't use limestone or marble rocks as their calcium will dissolve. Place the rocks and gravel to give different levels in the bottom of the tank. Fill with water by pouring into a cup in a saucer to avoid disturbance. Remove the cup and saucer and arrange the plants.

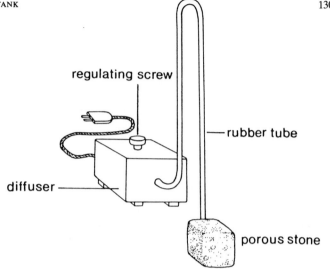

regulating screw

rubber tube

diffuser

porous stone

Aerator system for fish tank

Make sure they are clean (from a reputable supplier) and remove any dead leaves, then push into the gravel so that the crown is level with the surface of the gravel and the roots are buried. Should you want plants that need soil it is best to keep them in their pot and bury that in the gravel.

The most important point is *not* to put fish in for several days, or better still, two or three weeks, to allow the plants to root, the chlorine of the water to clear, and the bacterial nitrogen cycle to become established. An outside filter can be added. If you prefer an internal filter it has to be placed in the tank first, before the rocks and gravel are added. An aerator can be added later. If the tap water is excessively hard you will have to use rain water collected off a roof that will not contaminate it; for example, a glasshouse roof is ideal. Surface water in a river may contain fertiliser or pesticides that are dangerous.

The aim is to get bacteria established which deal with the dead organic material.

Fish are added (after a period of quarantine) by placing the container holding them in the tank water without allowing the waters to mix until the two are at the same temperature, and then tipping the container to allow the fish out into the tank. (See also Water).

A dip tube is used to remove larger pieces of debris. It works by putting one's finger over the end of the tube and inserting the other end into the water, and placing it over the debris. Then removing the finger allows water plus debris to flow in and up the tube. Place a finger over the end and remove tube and contents.

TAR ON FEET

Can cause serious inflammation in dogs and cats. It is best removed by dissolving it in oil or butter and removing the mixture with detergent.

TEETH

Mammals grow two sets of teeth. First, milk teeth when young which are shed to be replaced by permanent ones, which in most carnivores reach a maximum size, and in many herbivores keep growing throughout life as they wear down.

The age of horses and donkeys can be gauged by the appearance of the teeth.

The foal's first incisor appears at one week, the second at one month and the third at six months. The first permanent incisor, in the centre, erupts at 2½ years, the second at 3½ years the third at 4½ years, and the canine at 4½–5 years. The enamel disappears from the centre of the table of the first, second and third incisor teeth at 6, 7 and 8 years respectively. And at 7 years a hook appears on the end of the upper third incisor. The outline of the table of the incisors changes from oval to triangular at 11, 12 and 13 years in the first, second and third. Thereafter ageing is less accurately gauged.

The dog's milk teeth erupt at 4–6 weeks and they are replaced by permanent teeth at 4–6 months. Thereafter one can only guess age from appearance (the teeth are less bright and new-looking as the animal gets older).

The cat grows permanent teeth at 5–6 months old.

Because the teeth of horses and donkeys grow and wear, the wear can be uneven and it is relatively common for the molar teeth to require rasping. The outer edges of the upper molars and the inner edges of the lower become razor sharp and hurt the cheek and make chewing difficult. The animal may drop cuds (partly chewed pellets of food) from the mouth and appetite is poor and condition is lost. Sometimes food gets packed between two molars and begins to decay, causing infection and pain. The animal loses appetite and holds affected side tilted downward. Breath may smell bad. Occasionally a tooth is broken and begins to decay with similar symptoms.

Dogs and cats can break a canine or molar tooth and an abscess can develop at the root. From about six years old tartar begins to collect on the enamel and, if excessive, causes inflammation of the gums. It can be chipped and scraped off, leaving clean, shiny enamel exposed. Caries does not occur but packed food particles can cause inflammation around the tooth.

It is not uncommon, especially in dogs, for the first or 'milk' canines to be retained after six months and prevent the permanent canines from erupting. It is then necessary to have them removed.

Small herbivores can sometimes break one or both incisors on one jaw which allows the opposing incisors to grow excessively. If not noticed they may become so long as to prevent the animal closing its mouth, and so will stop chewing and cause emaciation and death.

TEMPERATURE

Of the body of the:

Horse is	38 °C (100.5°F)	Guinea pig	39.6°C (103.5°F)
Donkey	38.2°C (100.8°F)	Hamster	39.4°C (103°F)
Dog	38.4°C (101°F)	Gerbil	38 ° (100.5°F)
Cat	38.4°C (101°F)	Rat	27.5°C (99.8°)
Rabbit	40 °C (104°F)	Budgie	42.5°C (108°F)

Temperature is taken by inserting the thermometer into the rectum for ½ to 1 minute.

Tortoises are poikilothermic, or cold-blooded, which means they require an environment that is not too cold nor too hot. The range

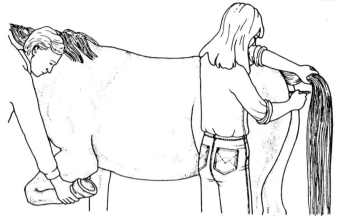

Restraint in order to take a horse's temperature

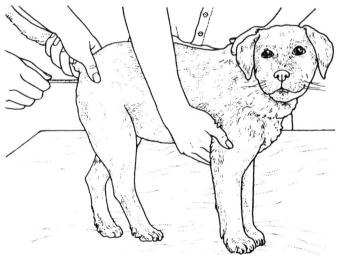

Taking a dog's temperature

should be 68°F to 85°F (20–29°C).

The body temperature of the tortoise should not drop below 65° (18°C) or it will become torpid. Too high an environmental temperature causes sudden fast movements, a lot of bathing, frequent short breaths (see also Heat Stroke). Too low a temperature causes slow movements, slow reactions and loss of appetite (see Housing and Accommodation).

A cold water aquarium does not require heating. Room temperature is satisfactory. Avoid the possibility of rapid temperature change. (See position of tank under Tank).

TENDONS

Join muscles with the bones at a distance from the muscle. They are strong and elastic but subject to injury by strain and wounds. Because they have a poor blood supply they are slow to heal and require plenty of rest (see Strain).

Severed tendons can be sutured and will heal. Consult your vet.

TETANUS

(Lockjaw) is a disease caused by a bacterium which produces a toxin that causes muscular spasms. Not only are they painful but spasms of the muscles used in respiration can cause death by asphyxia. The bacteria, which live in soil, enter through a wound which may be very small and unnoticeable.

Horses and donkeys are more susceptible than other species. The main symptoms are contraction spasms of the muscles of the face, tail, back and legs, and later many other voluntary muscles.

Treatment requires expert veterinary help.

There is a vaccine available.

Horses: Primary vaccination – 2 doses of vaccine 2 weeks apart.
          Booster vaccination – 1 dose after 12 months results in long-lasting immunity.
          Advisable to repeat at approximately two-year intervals.
Foals can be vaccinated at 3–4 months of age.

TICKS

Blood-sucking parasites whose bite is painless but many species cause transient diseases, some of them serious. They are among the largest ectoparasites of pets. They have eight legs and an abdomen that can dilate with blood when feeding. Afterwards they drop off until they are ready for the next feed, and they can survive for up to five years without feeding. They attach themselves to any passing host animal.

Treatment It is tempting to try to pull the tick off the animal but the mouth part can break and remain embedded in the skin and cause abscesses. It is wiser to wash, spray and dip the animal with a solution of insecticide. The recent insecticides are effective and the manufacturers' instructions should be followed exactly.

Ticks are sometimes found on tortoises, especially newly imported ones. They are found singly or in clusters clinging to the soft parts of the animal's body especially around the neck and rear limbs. They are about the size of a ladybird and grey/white with a reddish tinge at times. The mouth parts are buried in the body of the tortoise, so great care is needed in removing them as if the mouth parts break off and remain embedded suppuration can occur. It is best to dab the tick with methylated spirits and and it should slowly release its grip and may be carefully pulled away. Methylated spirits cannot be used around the eye or cloaca. Instead use liquid paraffin and wait ten minutes or so to remove ticks from those regions.

TIREDNESS

May be due to overweight, anaemia, leukaemia, or diabetes mellitus, and occurs in many serious diseases and heavy infestations of parasites.

Treatment depends on cause. Consult your vet.

Lethargy in tortoises can be caused by a low environmental temperature, faulty diet low in protein or vitamin A, faulty accommodation (uninteresting and boring), constipation, dehydration, worms, parasites, and disease. (See relevant section).

Tiredness or lassitude in fish is a sign of ill health. It may be caused by parasites or disease; ectoparasites, worms or infections such as tuberculosis may be the cause. It could be caused by poor oxygenation. If so the fish will be respiring fast and they may be gulping surface air or congregating near the aeration tube. Check the PH and smell the water for excess ammonia or a bad smell denoting that the nitrogen cycle has broken down (see Nitrites).

TONSILLITIS

Only of importance in dogs and cats. It is caused by infection. Symptoms are fever, loss of appetite and retching from time to time.

Treatment is to give antibiotics either by injection or by mouth. Your vet should be consulted.

TOXAEMIA

Means the accumulation of sufficient toxins in the blood to cause symptoms of illness. Toxins can be of external origin, for example, from the food; or of internal origin, from the breakdown of food in the digestive system; or they may be produced by certain bacteria multiplying in the body.

Symptoms are dullness, depression, normal or subnormal body temperature, the animal may lie down and refuse to get up, and it refuses food. Membranes become congested and not the normal pink colour. Later there may be vomiting and diarrhoea. It is a serious condition and the vet should be consulted at once.

TRACHEA

Or windpipe is lined with sensitive mucous membrane which, if stimulated by a foreign body or irritant smoke or gas, will cause coughing. The trachea cartilage may be injured but it is fairly robust. The lining can become infected (tracheitis) and this is usually associated with bronchitis.

TRANQUILLISERS

Used mainly to control savage, nervous or fractious animals for specific reasons such as after a shock, before examination or anaesthesia, or before trimming feet and nails and dressing painful wounds.

Only the more powerful tranquillisers have any real effect on animals and it is best to get professional advice as to when and how much to use.

TRAVEL
Animals travel well as a rule if they are accustomed to it from an early age. Otherwise, and for some particular individuals, it may cause much distress, even sufficient stress to precipitate shock and/or disease.

It is not recommended to use tranquillisers for calming an animal for travel unless prescribed by a vet. Get the animal used to the travelling box, make sure there is plenty of ventilation and circulation of air, and except for dogs and cats, give a light feed and adequate drinking water before the journey. Because dogs and cats often refuse to soil the box they refuse to pass urine in it and may go through agony. So it may be as well to withhold water for a few hours before the journey unless it is rather long. If the journey is long take them out of the box for exercise and to pass urine, and all other species should be watered and given a light feed to calm them.

See also Motion Sickness.

TREMBLING
May be due to nervousness, cold, fever and milk fever (eclampsia). Prolonged stress can also be responsible. Check the animal's body temperature and for other symptoms. Milk fever occurs after giving birth.

Accurate diagnosis is necessary.

TUBERCULOSIS
Not uncommon in fish. It resembles TB in man and animals. It causes a variety of symptoms – lassitude, loss of appetite and loss of weight. It can affect the skin, causing ulceration. When internal organs are affected nothing may be visible apart from the general symptoms listed above.

The disease will spread to other fish (it does not affect man) so the infected fish must be removed at once. Treatment with specific antibiotics used in human TB have been tried but with doubtful success.

TUMOURS

A type of slow-growing benign growth that can occur in almost any part of the body.

Your vet should be consulted if a lump develops.

Tumours can affect tortoises. They are not normally apparent to the lay person.

Fish are also susceptible to a variety of tumours and cancers in various organs. Treatment is not practical. Not enough is known. Some are considered to be hereditary.

TWITCHING

May be due to skin problems like parasites, flies, fleas, lice, mange, anal inflammation and allergy. It just might be poisoning or tetanus, but if so the animal will be showing other symptoms.

ULCERS

An area where the surface layers of the skin or mucous membranes are missing and a raw area is exposed that persists for long periods.

Ulcers of the skin are rare and not to be confused with eczema or dermatitis. They can sometimes result from infection of wounds. A so-called rodent ulcer in cats is a small red, raw area on the lip border.

Ulcers of the mucous membranes are less rare. They occur in the mouth, intestines, and surface of the eyeball. One cause of ulcers in the stomach and colon is stress in susceptible individuals. Several virus and fungal infections cause ulcers in the mouth.

It is necessary to consult a vet for diagnosis and treatment.

UNCONSCIOUSNESS

Results from collapse, shock, heat, stroke, accident and the terminal phase of serious disease. Injury to the head is the most likely. Heart failure and certain types of poisoning may also cause loss of consciousness. Contact your vet at once.

URAEMIA

The name of a group of symptoms caused by renal failure. Nitrogen-containing substances and other waste products build up because they are not excreted. There is also a lack of water, and of blood and body-fluid chemicals such as bicarbonate.

The main symptoms are those of gastro-enteritis. There may also be rapid breathing and either apathy, or excitement, or convulsions and coma.

Accurate diagnosis is necessary before correct treatment can be given. Consult your vet.

URETHRA

The tube carrying urine from the bladder to be voided.
Inflammation (urethritis) can be caused by infection or calculi.
Calculi are not common in most species except the male castrated cat. The calculi are sand-like granules that gradually occlude the urethra.

Occasionally in male dogs calculi form and lodge in the penis. They are like small stones.

Symptoms: the animal makes frequent and continuous attempts to pass urine and presses out only a few drops at a time. If left untreated, infection of the bladder and damage to the kidneys result.
See your vet as soon as possible for treatment.

URINE

Varies in appearance from species to species. It can also vary with diet and state of health.

Urine of horses and donkeys is cloudy, fairly strong-smelling, and yellowish. Colour and smell can vary, and account should be taken of the animal's state of health. Blood in the urine is abnormal and a vet should be consulted.

Urine of adult cats and dogs is also yellowish in colour and can be somewhat strong-smelling.

Small mammals pass smaller amounts of urine which will soon become strong-smelling if not removed.

Laboratory examination is required to learn anything of importance from the urine.

Difficulty in passing urine may be due to injury, calculi, infection of urethra or bladder, and enlarged prostate in the dog.

Incontinence may be a psychological problem. It can also be caused by infection, injury, and tumour in the bladder, and sometimes follows speying.

A vet should be consulted.

UTERUS

(The womb) may fill with pus (see Pyometra). It may become infected after giving birth. The usual causes are a retained afterbirth or a difficult birth that has injured the wall of the uterus.

In the mare and jenny retained afterbirth (the membrane in which the foal developed) is a most serious problem. It should be expelled between half an hour and an hour after the foal is born. If it hasn't come away within two hours, call your vet immediately, for in most cases it will become infected and cause toxaemia.

In dogs and cats there is a separate sac for each young one which comes away before the next baby is born. If one sac is retained it can set up an infection. As the mother often eats the sac, it is difficult to know. If in doubt call your vet.

The afterbirth can be retained in other species and the uterus become infected but it is less common. Symptoms are loss of appetite, loss of milk, fever and dullness.

Treatment is antibiotics to control the infection and an injection of a hormone to stimulate the uterus to expel the membrane.

VACCINATION

A method of protecting animals against those diseases for which there exists a reliable manufactured vaccine. Though some vaccines are made in a way that can be given by mouth, nearly all veterinary vaccines are administered by injection.

Each dose stimulates the animal to produce its own antibodies, but the immunity fades and so booster doses are required. Baby animals get antibodies from their mother which protect them for eight weeks. But those antibodies prevent the vaccination from having its full effect, so second and sometimes third doses are necessary when the first dose is given early in life.

Horses and donkeys have to be vaccinated against influenza: the Jockey Club requires all horses to be correctly vaccinated before being admitted to a point-to-point. Dogs can be vaccinated against distemper, parvo, canine hepatitis and leptospirosis, and all these vaccinations are recommended. Cats can be vaccinated against cat flu and feline enteritis (panleucopenia): and both are recommended but particularly the latter. Rabbits can be vaccinated against myxomatosis.

There are no vaccines available that can be recommended for other pets.

The recommended vaccination times are as follows:

Horse and donkey

   1st dose between 5 and 7 months of age

   2nd dose between 21 and 92 days after 1st dose

   Booster doses each year, not more than a year apart.

Dogs

   Distemper – 1st dose (optional) at 8 weeks old

                   2nd dose at 12 weeks old

                   Booster dose annually.

   Hepatitis and Leptospira – 1st dose at 12 weeks old

                                   2nd dose 14 days later

                                   Booster dose annually.

   Parvo – 1st dose at 8 weeks old

              2nd dose at 12 weeks old

              3rd dose at 20 weeks old

              Booster doses at 17–24 months old.

   These vaccines can be given together in the same injection.

Cats

   Feline Enteritis – 1st dose at 8–10 weeks old

                        2nd dose at 12 weeks old

                        Booster doses annually

   Feline rhinotracheitis (FVR)

   Feline calicivirus (FCD)

A combined vaccine for these two diseases may be given before 12 weeks of age if there is a definite risk.

   In this case: 1st dose at 9 weeks old

                    2nd dose 3 weeks later

                    3rd dose 3 weeks later

                    Booster doses may be given annually

Vaccination of all 3 diseases may be given in the same injection
Rabbits
    Myxomatosis – 1st dose at 12 weeks old
                   Booster dose annually

VAGINA

The entrance to the womb and is liable to infection contracted from
mating or after giving birth, and to tumours.

Symptoms are a white pus discharge that is usually partly mucus,
redness of the lining and perhaps dermatitis of the vulva.

Treatment: antibiotics given by injection or orally, or used locally
in the vagina. It is not serious though it may prevent conception. If
it persists consult your vet.

VIRUS

A very small ultra-microscopic germ that infects animals causing
disease. It is much smaller than a bacterium and can only be seen on
the electron microscope. (See also Vaccination and under disease
headings.)

VITAMINS

Chemicals that are essential items of a diet in very small amounts.
Deficiency can occur when owners make up the diet and use too
little variety and poor quality food. Manufactured diets from
reputable companies can be obtained for most species and are
balanced diets.

However, individual needs vary and young growing animals use
more in relation to their weight than adults. Also some chronic
diseases interfere with digestion and the uptake and utilisation of
vitamins so that more are required in the diet.

Symptoms of deficiency are:
Vitamin A – loss of appetite and weakness. If severe there may be
skin problems, night blindness and reduced natural resistance to
disease. But this is not likely to occur with available diets.
Vitamin B (thiamine) – loss of appetite, weakness and nervous
system problems. And if severe, there can be disturbance of the
digestive system. B1 is found in cereals so a diet of cooked meat and

refined carbohydrates can be deficient.

Vitamin B2 (riboflavin) is not likely to be lacking, but if so, there is weakness, loss of appetite and skin and nervous system disorders and corneal opacities.

Vitamin B6 (pyridoxine) is rarely if ever lacking from the diet. Nicotinamide may be deficient if the diet is low in meat and unrefined cereals. Loss of appetite, weakness and disorders of the digestive system result and also, sometimes, hyper-excitability.

Vitamin C Animals may not be receiving enough and become lame but it's uncommon.

Vitamin D may be deficient in the diet of fast-growing pups and rickets develops. (See Rickets).

Vitamin E can be lacking in the diet of cats and dogs if their diet contains too much fish or they are given too much cod liver oil. Deficiency causes muscle disorders and heart problems, and fatty-looking faeces.

Vitamin B12 deficiency causes loss of appetite, weakness and anaemia but it is rarely lacking in normal diets. Birds get the vitamin by eating their own faeces, and rabbits must be able to eat their own faeces or their digestion will not be normal and deficiency results.

There are many vitamin preparations available and the danger is in giving too much of some, which can also cause problems. Never exceed the recommendations of the manufacturer.

Tortoises require vitamins, which they will obtain from a good varied diet. Vitamin A is the one most likely to be deficient, which results in eye problems and loss of appetite. In winter it may be necessary to supplement the diet with added vitamins and minerals, and Vionate made by Squibb has been found most satisfactory. For dosage see manufacturer's recommendations.

VOMITING

The voidance of stomach contents. Some animals (bitches) will bring up stomach contents to feed their young. Some species vomit easily to get rid of irritating contents. Others, like the horse and donkey, rarely vomit.

Abnormal causes are gastritis; gastro-enteritis; obstruction of the digestive tract with foreign bodies, tumour, or narrowing of the lumen with scar tissue; poisons; inflammation of several organs, e.g. tonsillitis, hepatitis, nephritis, metritis, and pyometra; also a number of diseases can cause vomiting, such as distemper in dogs, hepatitis, etc. (See other sections in the book).

Treatment depends on the cause. If the animal is not depressed, has a normal temperature, and vomits only once or twice, it is only indigestion which will pass. If the animal shows other symptoms, consult your vet.

WARTS

Skin growths caused by a virus mainly in young animals. As a general rule immunity develops and they disappear as the animal gets older. They can be removed. (Remember the blood is infectious to other animals). Surgery can spread the warts on the animal.

Treatment: salicylic acid ointment will gradually 'burn' the wart away with little pain. It is applied daily after the area around the warts is cleaned. Don't apply the ointment to the skin. It will cause inflammation and perhaps loss of hair.

WASHING

Animals usually keep themselves clean. It is not wise to bath an animal too frequently for it removes the skin oils and can cause irritation. Always use a mild soap or detergent especially made for shampooing. Never use disinfectant soaps unless recommended by the vet. Rinse out all soap and detergent. If soapy water gets into the ear canals, be sure to dry them carefully. Dry the animal with towels and put it into a warm, draught-free room to dry out.

A hair dryer may be used on dogs and cats with care and so long as it doesn't cause distress.

WATER

Varies in its composition. Tap water is safe to drink but it will vary in hardness and it contains chlorine, which can injure or kill fish.

River and spring water can be safe but both can contain traces of nitrate fertiliser from farms, and even pesticides which are dangerous to fish in very small amounts.

Rain water collected from roofs can be contaminated.

The water in your fish tank should not be hard and its PH should be close to neutral. Tap water is safest provided it is allowed to stand until the chlorine it contains evaporates off. Temporary hardness can be removed by boiling, which will precipitate the salts. Permanent hardness can only be removed with chemical water softeners. It is unnecessary to remove hardness provided the PH is near neutral. It is more important to make sure the tank water contains enough oxygen by not having too many fish (see Tank). And to make sure the aerator is working if the tank has more fish than the surface area indicates. It is also important to make sure the water doesn't get too hot, or the temperature fluctuate rapidly (see Tank). Make sure the nitrogen cycle is working (see Nitrites), and that all food is eaten and dead plant leaves removed, for uneaten food and dead leaves may cause an increase in nitrites and poison the fish.

Remember that some treatments, for example with methylene blue or antibiotics, can kill the bacteria which break down nitrites and cause a build-up of toxic nitrites.

Most cases of stress in fish are due to problems with water: either it is too acid or too alkaline, or there is a build-up of ammonia or nitrites.

WEAKNESS
(See Tiredness).

WEANING
Normally occurs gradually. The mother entices and teaches the young to eat solid food. Dogs will at first vomit up solid food for the pups and later will bring in food for them. It is important to make food available for the young. Grass or hay for foals, milk and solid food for dogs and cats, and the normal diet for small herbivorous animals.

Weaning will take place slowly and naturally and the change over from mother's milk will not cause problems.

Horse and donkey foals are weaned at about one year of age.

Dogs and cats can be weaned at eight weeks, rabbits at six weeks, guinea pigs at three weeks (for they are born with eyes open and a full coat of hair); and small rodents – rats, gerbils and hamsters – are weaned at six weeks.

WEIGHT

Animals given a good diet and the space to exercise, and provided they are healthy, will maintain a weight in the normal range.

If the animal is overweight, diet and exercise must be examined (see Fat).

If it is underweight, thin or emaciated, yet the diet is adequate, there must be a disease problem – most probably worms (see Worms). Consult your vet if it is very thin.

For calculating the weight a tortoise should be, see section on Hibernation. Thin animals have very loose skin and large hollows where the hind legs enter the shell.

WIND
See Gas.

WOMB
See Uterus.

WORMS

There are two main types in pets in Britain, viz., round worms and tape worms.

Round Worms are by far the most serious group affecting pets. They vary in size from bordering microscopic to many inches long. Practically all organs of the body harbour the parasite, though in some organs, only briefly in the developing stage. They lay eggs, some species hundreds and others thousands per day, which pass out in the faeces and hatch into larvae which are picked up by the animal. The larvae migrate through the animal's body, growing and changing through four larval stages before becoming adult and settling in their specific site. Some species of worms will only infect one species of animal and will be killed if eaten by another species, hence the value of grazing sheep occasionally on a horse pasture.

Other species can affect more than one species of animal. Newly
hatched larvae are killed by sunshine, and to a lesser extent,
dryness. Eggs can be fairly resistant to disinfectants.

Horses and donkeys can be infested with stomach worms, thread
worms, pin worms, strongyles, ascarides, and lung worms.

Thread worms usually affect only foals, and pin worms and
ascarides affect the young animal mainly.

Ascarides can grow to 10 inches (25.4 cm.) long, and because
they migrate through the liver and lungs before settling in the bowel
they cause damage, and sometimes respiratory symptoms, and even
rupture of the bowel. Don't graze foals year after year on the same
pasture.

Strongyles are the most important round worm. The larvae cause
a lot of damage during migration through the body. Some cause
damage to the blood vessels supplying the bowels and are a
common cause of colic. Symptoms are depression, tiredness, loss of
weight, diarrhoea, colic, anaemia and fever when larvae are
migrating. Some of the smaller species cause nodules on the bowel.

One species of lung worm affects horses and donkeys. Horses are
fairly resistant but donkeys are not. Symptoms are loss of weight,
breathlessness on slight exercise, dry cough and lung sounds. There
are several fairly good treatments on the market. Pasture
management is important.

Treatment: there are several effective drugs on the market and a
faeces examination can help in choosing one. The other important
part of treatment is the timing and the pasture management.
Because these worms lay so many eggs there is little point in
treating an animal and turning it out on a heavily contaminated
pasture. Also several consecutive treatments at three or four week
intervals may be necessary for adequate control. Consult your vet,
especially for lung worm treatment and control.

Dogs and cats are susceptible to only one group – the ascarides –
in Britain. Toxocara canis affects dogs, Toxascaris mystax affects
cats and Toxascaris leonina affects both cats and dogs. They are all
white, round-bodied, and tapered at each end. Canis can grow to
three inches (7.6 cm.) long and the others to one or two inches
(2.5–5.8 cm.). Only on rare occasions are they passed out.

Symptoms are more rare in young animals. A large number
migrating through the lungs at one time will cause coughing. Main
symptoms are unthriftiness, rough coat, poor condition, pot belly,
perhaps anaemia, and in many cases nervous symptoms too.
Occasionally they may be so numerous as to cause intestinal
obstruction.

Treatment: there are several very effective drugs on the market.
Follow the instructions carefully.

Smaller mammals are rarely affected. Budgies and canaries are
also rarely affected.

Tape Worms are white, flat and segmented. The head hooks on to,
or is buried in, the wall of the bowel. Segments are formed from it
and each has reproductive organs which develop eggs. Segments are
shed, pass out in the faeces, and break up to release eggs which are
eaten by an intermediate host where some of the life cycle takes
place. Species are generally host-specific and infect the same species
of intermediate host.

Horses and donkeys are susceptible to two species. The worm
segments are short and very broad, but the worm is only about three
inches (7.6 cm.) long and lives in the bowel. They cause
unthriftiness, digestive troubles, and anaemia. The bowel wall may
become ulcerated and thickened. The intermediate host is a small
mite.

Dogs and cats are susceptible to two groups of species, one of
which can also infect children – Dipylidium. It is 6–18 inches long.
The intermediate host is the flea. But it is the larval flea that eats
the eggs, and as the larval flea develops, so does the larval
tapeworm until it becomes a cyst in the adult flea. Dogs and cats
become infected by eating fleas containing tape worm cysts.

The other group (taenia) contains several species. They are much
longer – 2–15 feet long (61 cm.–4.5 metres). They don't cause much
trouble in spite of their size. They absorb food so the animal has an
increased appetite but remains thin. Some species, however, can
cause digestive trouble. The intermediate hosts are mammals such
as rabbits, sheep, cattle, pigs, rats, and occasionally man, where
they form cysts which vary in size from pinhead to an inch (2.5 cm.)
or so depending on species of worm. When eaten by dogs or cats

these cysts release larvae which attach themselves to the bowel wall and develop into adult worms. Other small mammal pets can act as intermediate hosts.

Birds get tape worms but infection in budgies and canaries is rare.

Treatment for horses and donkeys is pasture management. There is no effective drug.

For dogs and cats there are effective drugs. However, because the head is embedded in the bowel wall it is difficult to kill, and if it survives it will continue to grow.

Follow manufacturer's instructions carefully or, better still, consult your vet.

Tortoises rarely get tapeworms. Round worms are often found and sometimes the infestation is large and causes problems – loss of weight, loss of appetite perhaps, and lethargy. Treatment with Cevamisole either by injection or by mouth works well. Consult your vet regarding dose. Before using medicine try giving sections of orange or orange juice.

Worms in the adult form do not cause problems to fish as a general rule. The larval forms of some worms do cause problems. Roundworm larvae can just be seen as red worms in the muscle tissue or internal organs. Fluke larvae are found in the skin, causing black spot and white grub in the eye: they are also found in the muscle tissue. Tapeworm larvae are found in the body cavity. There is no satisfactory treatment for any of these.

WOUNDS

Are breaks in the continuity of the skin or mucous membranes of the body. Damage to the tissues underneath the skin and damage to the skin without a break are dealt with under other headings – haematoma, bruising, burns, etc.

There are three main types – puncture, incision or cut, and laceration. Unless the wound is small it should be sutured if fresh and this means consulting your vet. First aid is important to prevent loss of blood and contamination of, and damage to, the wound.

Puncture wounds such as caused by a nail, a splinter of wood, a dog's canine or a cat's claw, can introduce germs and soon become infected, with serious results. The wound should be

cleaned, the hair clipped to prevent matting that could stop
drainage, and antibiotic ointment or powder applied. There is a
danger of tetanus in the horse and donkey, and of cellulitis (a
spreading abscess) in the cat and dog. If the wound is deep or at all
swollen consult your vet, as an injection of antibiotics and anti-
tetanus is indicated.

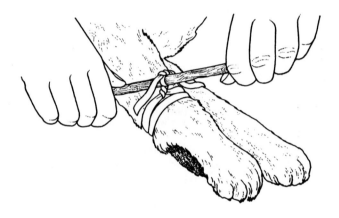

Putting a tourniquet on a cat's paw: tighten only until bleeding stops

Incisions or cuts may cause a lot of bleeding and may have
damaged tendons, muscles or nerves. If possible, using boiled water
and gauze, clean out any dirt, apply a pad of gauze and a layer of
cotton wool, and bandage, if possible, to stop the bleeding. If a
large artery is cut, apply a tourniquet above the cut (a tight bandage
twisted with a pencil or spoon handle till the spurting artery stops).
Seek veterinary help at once as it is dangerous to leave a tourniquet
on for more than half an hour.

A small wound can be cleaned with boiled water, the hair around
the edge clipped, antibiotic ointment or powder applied, then gauze
and cotton wool, and bandages as before. A large wound should be
sutured.

A lacerated wound should be seen by a vet or healing may be very slow and cause a lot of disfigurement. A wound that is not fresh will not be bleeding and the edges will be thickened and a serum discharge may be dripping away. Let the vet deal with it or it may get much worse. He will clean it, freshen the edges to stimulate healing, and may suture it.

The main problems delaying or preventing healing are infection, movement (a wound near a joint is constantly opened up), and interference (an animal rubbing, licking and biting at the area).

The main factors to assist healing after the vet has dealt with the wound are keeping the dressing in place and dry, stopping the animal interfering with the area, changing the dressing – but not too frequently, every two days is enough, and rest to reduce movement and a drag on the sutures.

Wounds are not uncommon in tortoises. They can become infected, suppurate and often smell badly. Some may get fly-blown and the maggots feed on the tissues and pus.

Bathe and clean the area thoroughly with a weak solution of Iodophor such as Betadine. Remove all larvae and dead tissue with forceps. If larvae are too deep to reach, fill hole in the skin with liquid paraffin. Bathe twice daily. If wound is large or doesn't improve rapidly it may be necessary to use antibiotics. Consult your vet.

Dog or cat bites cause puncture wounds in skin or shell. Not infrequently a garden fork is driven by mistake into the shell. This type of wound usually becomes infected and the animal soon loses its appetite and becomes lethargic. It is safer to seek expert help.

Fish are subject to injury but because of the strong, horny scales wounds are rarely deep. But slight injury can be followed by infection – often a fungal infection (see Skin).